`Jan `54

R Hear

SAINT AUGUSTINE

THE
STORY OF CHRIST

By GIOVANNI PAPINI

The Times Literary Supplement. The book is a live thing. Papini, the scoffer, was consumed with a burning desire to present Christ again to his world as a real living Being, and he has done it.

Father James Adderley in the *Daily Herald.* Everyone must read this book who wants to understand why Christian Social reformers are still almost the only ones who do not despair of a new world.

R. Ellis Roberts in *The Guardian.* It is the cry of the new age. It comes from the lips of a man who has trodden many paths.

J. C. Squire in *The Observer.* Any page taken at random will at once hold the attention.

HODDER & STOUGHTON

Photo

SAINT AUGUSTINE

From the painting by Botticelli, in the Chiesa d'Ognisanti, Florence

[Fro

SAINT AUGUSTINE

BY
GIOVANNI PAPINI

TRANSLATED BY MARY PRICHARD AGNETTI

HODDER AND STOUGHTON

LONDON   MCMXXX

Made and Printed in Great Britain for
Hodder and Stoughton Limited by
Hazell, Watson & Viney, Ltd., London and Aylesbury.

CONTENTS

5

6 C O N T E N T S

ILLUSTRATIONS

MY CONNECTION WITH SAINT AUGUSTINE

WHEN I was a child I had a kind and sprightly aunt who, in order to convey an idea of the assiduous application to study on the part of her son who had just begun to battle with simple Latin, used often to exclaim: " He writes as much as St. Augustine! "

This saying of hers is the only one that has remained in my memory of the numerous proverbs and mottoes that enlivened her conversation. The name of St. Augustine remained fixed in my mind, for at that time I too had begun to spill much ink and consume much paper for other purposes than those of school exercises. My imagination began to work in connection with the saint who had written so much as to become proverbial. Upon the stage of my obedient fancy I saw a man sitting in a closed room surrounded with books all of his own writing, with piles of papers and rolls of parchment beside him, and a pen-stand as full of quills as a quiver is of arrows. And when, after many years, I discovered, on the shelves of a library, the eleven ponderous volumes of the Order of St. Maur's edition of Augustine's works, I realized that my loquacious aunt had conveyed a correct impression of his activity.

A few years later, wandering alone one day in the

Uffizi Gallery, I was attracted by a small picture by our Sandro Botticelli. It represents an old man with a white beard, clad in a red robe, who is talking to a small boy on the shore of a sea as green and translucent as that in the Birth of Venus. The old man leans a little towards the child, who is on his knees beside a pool of water, holding a sort of bowl. I read the script beneath the picture: it represents St. Augustine, to whom a child is confessing his intention of emptying the sea. This strange episode enacted between hallowed age and ingenuous childhood in front of a shining, vast, and empty sea pleased me greatly, and never thereafter did I visit the gallery without pausing before this small panel, which is not, I believe, one of Sandro's best-known pictures.

It was about this time that I had to submit to being caged up in a school in Via Sant' Agostino over across the Arno. It was situated in an old convent whence the monks had been expelled, and the church connected with it turned into a gymnasium. And so, when I had scaled the poles (how my palms used to smart!) or was standing in line waiting for the order to attack the parallel bars, I could discern, high up aloft among the frescoes that related so many stories, a long, grey beard and a bishop's mitre which my fancy told me must surely belong to the author of the *Confessions*.

These are but childish memories that mean little, but to-day I regard them as the sign of my predestination to write this book.

As a matter of fact, I did not become acquainted with St. Augustine until I was nearing the end of my youth. An omnivorous reader like myself could not overlook the famous *Confessions*. Naturally I enjoyed what was human in them more than what was divine, but Augustine's romantic searchings of his own soul and his scathing and startling candidness took me by storm. I may say that before my return to Christ, St. Augustine, with Pascal, was the only Christian writer I read with a sense of admiration that was not solely intellectual, and during my struggle to break forth from the dungeons of pride and breathe the divine air of the Absolute, St. Augustine was of great help to me. I fancied there existed a resemblance between us; he also had been a man of letters and a lover of words, but at the same time a restless seeker after philosophies and truths, even to the point of being tempted by occultism; he also had been sensual and had sought fame. I resembled him in what was bad in him, of course, but after all I did resemble him. And the fact that a man of this sort, so like me in his weaknesses, had succeeded in achieving a second birth and in redeeming himself, was encouraging to me. The parallel, I would have it observed, ends here, for to-day I am as much like St. Augustine as a winged ant is like a condor. Be that as it may, however, I owe him a heavy debt of gratitude. Whereas at first I admired him as a writer, I now love him as a son loves his father, and venerate him as every Christian venerates a saint.

To this indebtedness and affection the present volume would bear witness. I am well aware that as a proof it is as ill-proportioned to the greatness of his genius as to the strength of my devotion, but it may nevertheless be judged not entirely useless and unworthy.

I have long contemplated writing this book, but engrossed as I have been in a work I deemed of far greater importance, I have always postponed its composition without actually relinquishing my intention, until finally my desire overcame me and forced me to fulfil my purpose.

III

This is not what to-day is termed a " romantic " biography, which is a biography hung around with fringes that are none the less fanciful for being plausible. I have endeavoured to write with straightforward simplicity both of the outward and of the inner life of the great African, always making it clear whether the facts given are well established or merely probable. Of course I have not simply paraphrased the *Confessions*, which, \indeed, bring us only to Augustine's thirty-third year, nor is this a full exposure of his thought, for to give but an idea of his philosophy, his theology, and his mysticism, several volumes far larger than this would be necessary.

My chief concern has been to write the *story of a soul*, and even the allusions to his vast labours are but examples necessary for a better understanding of his spiritual nature and to convey a more adequate idea of his greatness. I am no theologian, nor could I, without incurring grave risk, have ventured into the " forest dense and living " of his system; I have written as an artist and a Christian, not as a patrologist or scholastic.

Yet I do feel that the book contains some things which are new. I have neither concealed nor veiled any of the faults of Augustine's youth, differing herein from certain well-meaning but mistaken encomiasts who seek to reduce to naught the peccability of saints and converts, without pausing to consider that it is precisely in the fact that they have succeeded in rising from the depths of sin and soaring to the stars that their glory resides and that the power of Grace is made manifest.

The deeper the valley, the stronger the light upon the heights.

GIOVANNI PAPINI.

CHAPTER I

THE NUMIDIAN

To begin with, Aurelius Augustinus was a Numidian. If the fact of his nationality be lost sight of, certain aspects of his psychology must remain incomprehensible.

Roman Africa was Roman in name and government but not in its inhabitants. Roman colonists and immigrants were always few in number even after the defeat of Carthage. The names of the gods and of the people became latinized because Latin was the language of the masters and of commerce, but the majority of those who dwelt in the houses and trod the streets remained of African blood, and the Punic language was spoken until the sixth century, perhaps even until the Islamic invasion.

Augustine was certainly familiar with the Punic tongue, which with Latin was the language of his childhood, and Punic words actually occur here and there in his writings. Once when certain barbaric forms of native words were being ridiculed in his presence, he came to the defence of the language of his fathers, declaring that an African speaking to Africans should no more blush for his native tongue than for the land of his birth itself. In his old age he betrayed, perhaps all unconsciously, a remnant of

14

African patriotism when, in telling of the Punic wars in his *De Civitate Dei,* he placed Carthage on an equal footing with Rome both as regards power and glory, and his epic description of the descent of Hannibal is vaguely tinged with personal satisfaction.

These conditions notwithstanding, Africa gave pagan Rome many of her most famous authors, from the comic Terence to the magic Apuleius, and to Christian Rome Africa gave many of her doctors and saints, from Cyprian and Tertullian to our own Augustine. This vast continent, which was termed barbaric and dark, has had its part, and that an important one, in the spiritual history of mankind. Light came to Europe not from the Orient alone but from the South as well. The most remote and enduring civilization the world has known was developed in Africa; in Africa one of the most heroic and zealous churches of early Christianity came into being. From Africa came Neo-Platonic thought; from Africa the first perfect experiment in monasticism. Just as ancient Italy appeased her hunger with the corn of Egypt and Lybia, so throughout the ten centuries of the Middle Ages did the whole of Christianity feed upon the thoughts that had emanated from the fertile, lucid, and generous brain of an African from Tagaste.

To ancient geographers Africa was but the mys-

terious lair of lions and horned serpents; later on to
Europeans it became a very hive of corsairs, a breed-
ing-place for slaves; in our own day it is a source of
cotton, rubber, and the black flesh that becomes
food for cannon. But to the Christian it has ever
been and still remains the land of Aurelius Augustinus.

He was descended from those fierce Numidians
who, for long years, under the leadership of Jugurtha,
withstood the power of Rome and the genius of
Marius and Sulla; and perhaps when, in the opening
chapters of his *City of God*, Augustine penned his
denunciation of Roman rapacity and ruthless lust of
conquest, he was unconsciously influenced by the
stirrings within him of some remnant of the age-old
rancour of his decimated and subjugated ancestors.

The word *Numidian* would appear to be but a
derivative of *nomad*. Conquered and civilized
the nomads finally settled in the towns and ports;
but something of those early wanderings in search of
fortune and sustenance remained in the hot blood of
Augustine. Although he did not travel far in person—his journeyings being mainly between Tagaste
and Cassiciacum—his enquiring spirit roamed far
afield: from Cicero to Mani, from Mani to Carneades, from Carneades to Plotinus, from Plotinus to
St. Ambrose and finally to St. Paul, who led him to
the hermit's cave and the kingdom of Christ.

Throughout antiquity the Africans bore an undoubtedly well-deserved reputation for excessive licentiousness. Justinian, for example, wrote of Hannibal that so chaste did he remain in the midst of a horde of slaves and prisoners that it was difficult to believe him a native of Africa. From early adolescence Augustine displayed strongly voluptuous tendencies, and at the very moment of his conversion these tendencies seemed to him to be one of the greatest impediments in his path.

This race, however, was also religious, and its religion, although coarse and fierce, offered a more favourable preparation for the complete understanding of Christianity than that of the Romans. The Numidians had embraced the Phœnician religion—an Asiatic creed—which in one essential—its doctrine of absolute submission to the Divine Will—was in direct opposition to paganism. To the Romans religion was a species of legal contract between man and the gods. Man performed certain rites and uttered certain words at given times, and in exchange, if they were honest, the gods were bound to grant such benefits as they had promised. It was still the primitive, necromantic conception according to which, by means of a given ceremonial, certain individuals were empowered to violate the will of the divine forces of nature and force the hand of the gods themselves. In Rome frenzied sorcerers had

2

become public officials and sacred notaries, but the
principle remained unaltered.   On the other hand
the Punic religion, that of Augustine's forbears,
taught obedience and submission to the will of Baal
who, under the name of Saturn, had assumed the first
place among the gods, which in itself was a step towards monotheism.   Christianity therefore, wherein
they recognized the superior religiosity of submission
to the Divine Will as opposed to the challenge by
means of necromancy, made quick appeal to the
Africans, and was readily embraced by them.   In
Augustine's conception of the absolute supremacy of
the Divine Will, which underlies his theory of Grace,
I seem to trace the workings within him of this
Punic leaven.   God can accomplish all things, can
even save sinners, whereas man unaided can accomplish nothing.   In Pelagius he perceived, besides the
Stoic error, the pride that was the attribute of Roman
necromancy, the presumption of the creature to
power over the Creator.

The name of one of the faithful has been found
in a Punic inscription.   It is *Kelbilim,* which means
" hound of the divinity."   This name might well
have belonged to Augustine, who served his one
Lord indefatigably for more than forty years, and
stood boldly forth against all enemies of Christ and
His Church.

As ardent as the sun of his native land, sensual and

passionate like all of his race, his thought and writings
rich in *vigor igneus,* Augustine is the greatest of all
Africans.   Although he wrote in the language of
Virgil and was guided by Platonic thought until the
Hebrew Paul threw open to him the realms of light,
in certain characteristics he remained an African to
the end of his days.

The instruments, moreover, that gradually led
him to salvation were destined to come to Augustine
the African out of Africa.   Apuleius the Numidian
first inspired him with a taste for Platonic mysticism; Platonius the Egyptian revealed God to him
as a pure spirit; the example of Victorinus the African strengthened his desire to give himself up to
Christ, and finally another African, Pontitianus, by
acquainting him with the heroic life of Anthony of
Egypt, drove him, still reluctant, to the baptismal
font.

CHAPTER II

THE TWO SEEDS

JEAN PAUL RICHTER tells us that those who are born on a Sunday are destined to accomplish great things. Aurelius Augustinus is a proof of this somewhat dubious rule, for the thirteenth of November of the year 354, when Monica, wife of Patricius, bore him, was indeed a Sunday.

At that time Constantius II was reigning, having become sole ruler of the empire in the preceding year; and at the very moment of Augustine's birth Constantius was intent upon the execution at Pola of no less a personage than a Cæsar—of Gallus, his cousin, and nephew of Constantine the Great. In Rome the rudder of Peter's Church was held by the thirty-first of his successors, that St. Liberius, the builder of Santa Maria Maggiore, who, a year later, was destined to suffer banishment to Thrace at the hands of the Emperor, for the glorious crime of refusing to condemn St. Athanasius.

Thus, while a Cæsar was being done to death in Istria, a saint was being born at Tagaste, a small town of Numidia near Madaura. His mother was a Christian of Christian descent, but his father was a pagan, and not until long afterwards, yielding probably to his wife's entreaties, did he become a catechumen, and only on his deathbed did he receive baptism. In accordance with the custom of the times, the infant Augustine was left unbaptized, as if the cleansing waters were to be reserved as a reward for his famous victory achieved in the prime of his life at the age of thirty-three. At his birth, however, his mother signed him with the cross and touched his tongue with salt. From the beginning maternal affection had enrolled him in the army of Christ, but he was not destined to take his place in the line of battle until his youth was already nearly spent.

Of his father Patricius we know but little. Possidius says he was a magistrate, and he certainly held some property—perhaps a vineyard or a small farm —for in later years Augustine wrote of having liquidated his " very small patrimony " that he might bestow it in alms on the poor. Patricius was not sufficiently well off to have sent his son away to school had not Romanianus—a prominent man in the small town of Tagaste—afforded generous aid. But it was the father's ambitious determination to equip Augustine with an education, in the hope that a fine fortune would result. In his *Confessions* Augustine asserts that his parent's sole purpose in forcing him to submit to the torture of school life was " to satisfy his own insatiable avidity of copious gain and inglorious fame."

One fact alone appears well established among the rare memories of his father which the son chronicled

with grave circumspection—that Augustine found
it impossible to love him. He dwells on the fact that
both Patricius and Monica laughed at the strokes his
master dealt him, while to the boy this punishment
was an intolerable humiliation. He further recalls
that once when he went with his father to bathe at
the Thermæ, Patricius noticed signs of approaching
virility in the lad, and hastened home, greatly delighted, to impart his news to Monica as a promise
of coming happiness.

This incident is sufficient to show how completely
the provincial magistrate was dominated by sexual
considerations, a burdensome legacy to pass on to his
son, and one against which that son was destined to
struggle for many years. That Patricius was addicted
to carnal pleasures to the point of repeated unfaith-
fulness to Monica may be gathered from the testimony of Augustine himself who, when writing in
praise of his mother, says that she tolerated the *cubilis
iniurias* of her husband—his frequent offences against
the sanctity of the marriage bed.

His son adds that Patricius was extremely kind-
hearted, but at the same time subject to fits of rage,
when he would become so violent that Monica's
friends marvelled that she did not show traces of
blows inflicted by " so fierce a spouse." He died in 371
when Augustine was seventeen, probably still in the
prime of life, for his wife was but forty at the time.

Augustine did not love him, nor was it possible he should love one of Patricius' temperament. The son was well aware that the passions—lust, ambition, and greed of gain—which it would cost him so fierce a struggle to conquer, had come to him from his father. Augustine became what he is and what he will remain to all eternity—a saint—only by suppressing in himself all that was of his father. He is the son of Monica and of Grace. Patricius was but the instrument of sin that was necessary to clothe his spirit in flesh.

The tenderness Augustine evinced for Monica was a very different matter. In common with the majority of great men he owed to his mother the best attributes of his heart and perhaps also of his intellect. Whereas of his father he speaks grudgingly and never with any affection, concerning Monica he penned long pages which rank among the most fervent and glowing of his compositions. These are perhaps the finest pages ever written by a son in honour of his mother. If Monica bore a saint to the Church it may well be said, to use Dante's conception in another sense, that she was indeed the daughter of her own son, for from him and from him alone came the convincing testimony which led the Church to elevate the widow of Patricius to membership in the family of saints; and only the Christian heart can picture the ineffable sweetness of the first meeting in the peace and glory of Paradise between this mother and her aged son.

Not that Monica was perfect and a saint from her infancy. Brought up by a grey-haired and sternly uncompromising serving-woman, who even measured out to her the water wherewith to quench her thirst, Monica later acquired a liking, most unbecoming in a maiden, for the thick wine of Numidia that tastes of violets and wasps. Fortunately another maidservant, less austere but with a glib tongue, discovering the girl one day in the dim cellar, had words with her, and hurled at her the name of *meribibula,* which literally translated means a tippler or a sot. The one word sufficed to cure her.

Monica became a wife at an early age (if we consider the prevailing customs and the climate we may conclude that she married at fourteen or fifteen), and she succeeded in gaining and holding her husband's affection. Conjugal infidelity does not always destroy a husband's love for his wife; indeed, it would sometimes appear to have the effect of reviving it, and Monica's success with her lord is not surprising. What is more so is that she ingratiated herself with her mother-in-law as well. This lady, influenced by the malicious gossip of servants, had begun by hating the young wife, who, however, by dint of much gentleness, docility, and persevering endurance, managed so cleverly that at last the old woman herself ordered her son to have the slandering servants flogged, and henceforth the two women lived in perfect concord.

Even before she achieved saintliness Monica had been a young woman of great good sense, and of this her attitude towards her husband is proof sufficient. When his fits of rage were upon him she would leave him, quietly and without a word, to storm and curse until his passion was spent, and when presently his dark countenance assumed a milder expression, she would explain to him with great gentleness how and wherein he had erred. Not always, probably, were poor Patricius' ragings entirely unjustified, but his great fault was that he stormed too fiercely and brutally. Nevertheless his wise and patient wife, while living under the same roof with a husband so violent, managed so cleverly that not only was she herself never struck, but she also maintained peace in the household. Her powers of endurance had doubtless been strengthened by the lessons in humility she had received in childhood both in her own home and from the Church, but much was due also to her natural gentleness and keen intelligence.

She agreed with her husband in his desire that Augustine should study, and she could smile at his despair when his back was smarting from the rod. She had at that time no hopes of sanctity for him; her ambition did not soar to such heights, but she did desire for him the honourable and lucrative career of a professor of literature. The wise African wished her son to achieve wealth and fame, and in this one cannot but sympathize with her. On the other hand these ambitions, both paternal and maternal, served to promote the son's attainment of that fame which will endure for ever; for if Augustine had been left to idle away his youth in the streets and meadows in and around Tagaste he would never have become the sage who used his learning to illumine the wonderful faith of the ignorant.

Devoted to Christ and chaste by nature—her son more than once stressed the fact that she remained the wife of but one man, and this not of necessity, for she became a widow when still young—Monica was the very opposite of Patricius, that lukewarm pagan and reluctant Christian, who at bottom was ever perhaps an unbeliever and was most certainly an ardent sensualist. On becoming aware that her son was entering upon the perilous age of puberty, and alarmed, as she might well be, by his likeness to his father, Monica secretly exhorted the lad, for the love of God, to flee from all forms of fornication, and above all things not to render himself guilty of adultery. To this second of his mother's commands at least Augustine lent obedience.

Later on we shall find the continuous traces of her tears on the sinful path the young Augustine was pursuing, and we shall see what part, at certain

moments of supernatural exaltation, this grieving
woman—despairing yet ever hopeful—had in her
son's return to the Faith.   But now that Augustine
has reached the close of his childhood, we must henceforth bear in mind the fact of his dual heredity,
which explains certain inconsistencies in his character,
many of his temperamental contrasts and, in a large
measure, those fierce struggles between his two selves
that ended only in the garden at Milan.   Fourteen
centuries before Goethe our African felt within him
the co-existence of more than one spirit, and while
his final victory routed what was anti-Christian in
one of them—the spirit of his father—yet he retained
to the end a dualism which is reflected in the form
if not in the substance of his thought.   His nature
harboured both the unbridled sensuality of his father
and the gentle mysticism of his mother.   There dwelt
within him one who was avid of praise and one who
humbly mortified the flesh.   He possessed a sensibility
so acute and subtle as to render him conscious alike
of the world's remotest aspects and of the minutest
fibres of the soul.   His were also a well-balanced judgment and a sagacity that was pondered and human.
An inclination towards redundancy in rhetoric, which
culture had intensified, was balanced by an easy pre-
cision of expression that flowered in angelic and evan-
gelic simplicity.   There was within him a tangle of
seething, overflowing passions, yet he was also pos-

sessed of the power to raise himself to the *templa serena* of metaphysics.

Augustine owed this radical division of the ego to his parents—a division that often added richness to his life and works, but that also at times appeared as the clashing of heaven and hell within him. No wonder that, unconsciously swayed by these conflicting elements, he remained stranded for nine years in the dualistic heresy of Manichæism.

CHAPTER III

THE SINS OF INNOCENCE

UNLIKE other autobiographies, in writing the story of his soul Augustine was not content to begin with his first childish recollections. His craving for knowledge of the depths reached out beyond the bounds of memory. So lively was his sense of the infinite value of every immortal soul that he would fain know the origin of that which dwelt in his own flesh, and he was impatient to discover what he had been before being, before assuming visible shape on the day of his birth.

Although he is but " dust and ashes " he feels the need of ascertaining whence he came to enter into " this dying life or living death," and the fact that he is unable to solve the mystery does not give him pause. At least he will reconstruct the story of his infancy by means of his parent's reminiscences and his own knowledge of other children—the story of the life of which he was totally unconscious, of which he has no personal memory. He sees himself at his mother's and at his nurse's breast, and he imagines— albeit the fancy is rather of the poet than of the Christian—that the Almighty Himself has filled these breasts in order that the women, while finding relief themselves, may nurture him.

He tells of his first smile, his first whimperings, his

first consciousness of the outside world; of when he first distinguished between himself and others, and how he avenged himself by crying when his guardians opposed his will. Through studying other children and, in fancy, seeing himself in them, he came to recognize the traces of original sin in that state which common ignorance terms the " age of innocence."

Augustine did not wait for Freud to discover that the child from its mother's womb is less pure than most people believe. This Jewish alienist, who is an unbeliever even in his own synagogue, who glories in the well-deserved reputation of a scavenger of souls, but who, all unconsciously, has provided Christian apologists with fresh proofs of the existence of original sin and of the reasons for confession, flatters himself he has discovered what Augustine had clearly set forth and proved fifteen centuries earlier. Augustine had even noted the antagonism that may prevail between twin infants while still at the breast, and that even in infancy obscure criminal instincts may be apparent. " Innocence resides in the weakness of the infant members, not in the infant soul."

If childhood did not seem to him free from sin, neither did it seem a happy time. " Who would not be appalled," he writes in his *City of God*, " at the proposal to live through his infancy again, and would not rather choose death? " In his *De Peccatorum Meritis* he dwells on the brutish torpor in which children are immersed during their earliest years, seeing in it one of the effects of original sin.   How terrible if they should always remain in this sad and helpless state!   This age, which is regarded by many as the most blissful, a remnant, as it were, of Paradise, always seemed to Augustine a very Hades.   When he was six this Hades assumed the shape of school—of the grammar school at Tagaste—and the master with his rod was chief demon!

Augustine could not understand why he must study and obey his elders.   This lad, destined soon to become a clever student, later a learned teacher, and finally an indefatigable and respected master, began by hating books and schools, and what most keenly humiliated and distressed him was the teacher's birchings, not so much on account of the physical suffering incurred as because they aroused in him a sense of atrocious injustice.   These birchings, however, served to open to him the road to prayer, for he began at that time to beseech God to spare him these punishments, praying hard enough to " sever the ligaments of his tongue."   It was a childish manner of prayer and a coarse and egotistical form of devotion, but it was prayer for all that.   He was beginning to realize that he had but one ally, one hope in all the world—the Lord alone.

All of his early studies irked him—reading, writing, reckoning, but above all, when he was a little older,

Greek and mathematics. He never thoroughly mastered Greek, whereas he soon became enamoured of the virile and harmonious beauty of Latin. When declaiming the lament of Dido abandoned, he would be moved to tears by Virgil's lines, for his was a spirit destined to be in love with love.

Children's games of all sorts appealed to him far more strongly than study, and as an old man he complained that his elders had used the whip to keep him away from them, for, he observes, although the chief amusement of adults is called " trading," is it not also a game, and one far less innocent than the game of ball? Even in these childish pastimes his pride was such that he must always win at any cost, and if he found himself losing he was not above cheating in order to remain victor.

However, he was not merely what we should call a " sport addict," for he was also immensely fond of mimes and comedies; so fond indeed that, not content with frequenting the theatre, he and some of his companions must practise acting as well. Before becoming a rhetorician Augustine was an amateur actor, and the indulgence of this childish but absorbing passion soon led him into two forms of grievous sin —lying and stealing. He himself confesses to the " innumerable lies " wherewith he eluded the vigilance of masters and parents, and to his thieving, from the store-room, of the wherewithal to purchase the complicity and help of the boys who were his fellow-actors or partners in his games. Even when he had left childhood behind and attained the age of sixteen the hateful vice of peculation still clung to him, not because he desired to enjoy the fruits of his act himself, but that he might display his daring and ingratiate himself with his companions in idleness.

How eloquent he waxes as an old man, in his remorse for the stripping of a pear-tree in an orchard at Tagaste! And how deeply, in retrospect, does he probe the depths of his soul in his desire to explain to his own satisfaction a crime, small in itself, but so appalingly " gratuitous "!

At that time he had not yet lost his faith in Jesus. Once a congestion of the lungs threw him into so high a fever that his life was in danger, and he begged urgently for baptism. His mother was about to comply with his wish when he recovered. Hereupon the administration of the sacrament was postponed, perhaps because Monica, knowing him inclined to vice, feared his sins would weigh more heavily against him if committed after he had received the cleansing waters.

In reviewing his life Augustine saw this delay as unjust. To say " Let him go on," meaning " Let him continue to defile himself, for he is still unbaptized," seemed to him as absurd as to say of a wounded man,

" Let him suffer fresh wounds, for he is not yet healed."

But baptism was still withheld, and Augustine's youth could continue to be evil without the added sin of sacrilege. Thus on the threshold of adolescence we find him a rebellious scholar, a zealous comedian, a cheat, a liar, and a thief—in a word, a thorough good-for-nothing. But worse was to come, and the outbreak was near at hand.

CHAPTER IV

THE PRAYER OF LUCIUS APULEIUS

As the child developed into the youth Augustine's aversion to study lessened. He began indeed to be so fond of reading and especially of his beloved Virgil that he confesses he would have wept had he been deprived of the volumes.

He now became conscious that he possessed those qualities which are necessary in order to shine in the realms of rhetoric—" a good memory and facility of expression." He was also beginning to achieve success at school, and certain recitations delivered by him for the benefit of his fellow-students and of some of his youthful companions were received with enthusiastic applause. He was becoming so pedantic, however, that to be guilty of a barbarism caused him more acute suffering than to commit a sin, and he was always greatly chagrined if his fellow-students did not happen to fall into the same error. In short, Augustine was a youth of promise, of such promise that his father's complacent fancy already pictured him as becoming what Fronto had been to Cirta and Apuleius to Madaura—a famous teacher who, later on, would betake himself to Rome, accumulate sesterces by the bushel and eventually, perhaps, even attain to the imperial *curia*. So precocious a youth had nothing more to learn at Tagaste's modest school, and Patricius, having managed to scrape together the necessary funds, decided to send his son to Madaura, that he might there acquire eloquence and a knowledge of classic literature.

At that time Augustine must have been fourteen or fifteen years of age, and he was naturally delighted to escape from maternal vigilance and reside in a town which, compared with Tagaste, must have seemed a large city. Madaura was but a few miles distant, and to the educated its chief claim to renown resided in the fact that it had been the birthplace of Lucius Apuleius, author of the *Metamorphoses* or *Golden Ass*, of an *Apologia* that at bottom is but a defence of necromancy, of the *Floridæ*, and of works on Socrates and Plato. He was one of the most adventurous spirits of the second century, and the most original stylist produced by Africa before Tertullian. He had studied all the different philosophies, had been initiated in all the mysteries, had travelled half round the world, had been held in consideration at Rome, and had died at last in Carthage, full of honours.

It was not possible that the young Augustine should fail to study and admire the works of one whom his own father and all his teachers had pointed out as a model, especially as he was himself setting out upon the same path in life and was living in Apuleius' own city, where the memory of the prolific writer was more vivid than anywhere else. In fact, Augustine often alludes to Apuleius in his *City of God*, pronouncing the *De Magia copiosissima et disertissima oratio*, recalling the *Golden Ass*, making use of the author's notes on demons in a letter he wrote to Marcellinus in 412, citing him as an example in demonstrating the importance of the art of magic.

It is my firm conviction that the influence of Apuleius was the first that bore upon Augustine's mind, if but vaguely perhaps, still sufficiently to predispose him not only to the study of philosophy and to the reception of the impression Cicero's *Hortensius* would make upon him a few years later, but also to deeper reflection upon the divine mysteries. Apuleius was no ordinary man, no mere rhetorician, and still less, like so many of his contemporaries, an arid rationalist or a sneering sceptic. In the *De Magia* he defends not only magic but philosophy as well, and this in accents of unusual sincerity. His knowledge of Socratic, Platonic, and Aristotelian thought was far from superficial, and he had acquired it at the sacred fountain-head—beneath the colonnades of Athens. That half-grotesque, half-gruesome apparition, the *Golden Ass* itself, ends its career with a prayer to the goddess which one feels is sincere and which, with some slight alterations, might well have been pronounced by Christian lips. Apuleius was a sophist, but he was also a mystic. " There is in him," writes an historian of Latin literature, " a sincerity, an ardour of philosophic and religious conviction, an aspiring towards the infinite mystery that carries one far beyond such harmless pedants as Fronto and Aulus Gellius, and leads one nearly to Christianity. . . . He comes from the Schools and draws nearer to the Church; he does not enter indeed, but he stands on the threshold."

Such an author, revealed to the youthful Augustine precisely at this moment of youthful intellectual avidity, could not but leave his mark on the student's spirit. Between these two there existed a natural affinity which paved the way for this influence. They were both lovers of beauty in speech, of subtlety in thought; both were gifted with insight, prescience, and faith; both, in a word, were mystics.

If Apuleius was a magician or rather a dabbler in magic, Augustine also, at a later date, made a study of astrology, and not until many years afterwards, in Milan, did he succeed in detaching himself from it entirely.

In my opinion it was Apuleius who first freed Augustine from the worship of language for its own sake and of literature as such. That breath of mystery which emanates from his works awoke in the Numidian student the buried remains of Punic religiosity and enabled him to sense more deeply the mystery of Christianity.

Perhaps on one of Madaura's mild evenings the future saint may have read in the *Golden Ass* that prayer which would remind him of words that were often upon his mother's lips: "Holy and perpetual refuge of humanity, munificent dispenser of favours to mortals, ever dost Thou succour the wretched with maternal affection. Not a day passes, not a night, not a single minute wherein Thou dost not grant Thy protection to man. . . ."

But the influence of Madaura's Platonic philosopher was soon wrecked in the storm of carnal excess by which Augustine was swept in the following year. It was that much-slandered haranguer of Arpinum who, later on, was destined to reawaken in him the love of pure thought.

CHAPTER V

THE ONSLAUGHT OF PUBERTY

PATRICIUS, a small land-owner of meagre resources, had allowed his ambition to blind him to the inadequacy of his means, and he soon became aware of his inability to defray his son's expenses at Madaura. Augustine, therefore, was obliged to return to his home, and at Tagaste he idled away one whole year, the sixteenth of his life, in the company of dissolute companions and at the mercy of his own proclivities.

His father was not discouraged, however, and exerted himself to obtain the money necessary to keep the lad at a more famous school in Carthage, a far more important city. Meanwhile Augustine, who had nothing more to learn from the teachers at Tagaste, was running wild, and no longer restrained by the discipline of study, he quickly succumbed beneath the onslaught of puberty.

He was at a dangerous age. In that sun-scorched land virile development is precocious. To these circumstances must be added the facts of his paternal heredity, his own passionate nature, evil examples— even in his own family—and the daily temptations his state of freedom afforded. The seething impulse of sex became master of the youth, and from the age of sixteen until he was two-and-thirty Augustine, ever attracted by lasciviousness, remained a true voluptuary.

He himself has said so not once but repeatedly and with deep contrition; and to my mind those critics err who seek to place his confessions, made at a ripe age, in the light of intentional exaggerations due to Christian remorse. Why should this saint, who never fails to convey the most convincing sense of veracity, declare himself more guilty than he really was by accusing himself of a sin more shameful than any other in the eyes of his newly acquired brethren? This would have been to lie gratuitously, whereas in his words there is no trace of that decadent pose assumed by certain moderns who court shameful celebrity by boasting of horrors of which, as a matter of fact, they are not guilty.

Anyone who reads with attention the second and third books of the *Confessions* must perceive that the virulence of carnal desire was very strong in Augustine during this period. His biographers have hitherto sought to gloss over this storm of sensuality, and have cast a veil over one form of vice in which he indulged that is more repugnant than any other, the existence of which, however, is clearly demonstrated by his own accounts. In Augustine there abode both a satyr and an angel, and these years belonged essentially to the satyr, whereas the last four-and-forty years of his life were ruled by the angel.

Nor can these shameful conditions of his youth de-
tract from his future sanctity, as some over-fastidious
persons hold; for the fouler the depths of the abyss
from which he was dragged to be transfigured in celestial radiance, the more entirely supernatural must the
prodigy of Grace appear.

When he tells us of his " turpitude and carnal corruption," of the " hellish voluptuousness of his adolescence," and relates how he lost himself " in the forest
of dark and diverse passions," we are bound to believe that he is not exaggerating. Unfortunately he
indulged in forms of passion other than the natural.
The texts speak plainly enough; there is no need to
read between the lines.

" What delighted me more," says Augustine, " than
to love and be loved? But I overstepped those
bounds that separate one soul from another and
within which the light of chaste friendship shines
brightly. Rather did the loathsome concupiscence
of the flesh and my state of seething puberty envelop
and blind my spirit with vapours that *prevented me
from distinguishing between serene affection and
black lasciviousness,* both of which flamed within
me, forcing me, in my youth and weakness, into the
abyss of lustfulness and plunging me up to the neck
in sin." Here, couched in decent language, we have
an unequivocal allusion to the degradation of friendship that has degenerated into lasciviousness and abides

in it. Augustine would not talk of " friendship "
were he alluding to women or girls. When he speaks
of friends he is always referring to men, nor did
the modern custom then exist of calling a mistress
by the name of friend. Probably in a small town
like Tagaste it was no easy matter for an impecuni-
ous, inexperienced, and very young man like Augustine to carry on intrigues with women, whereas familiar intercourse with male companions of his own
age was neither forbidden nor likely to arouse suspicion.

If anyone still doubts let him read the opening
paragraphs of the third book: " I yearned to love and
to be loved, and my delight herein was greatest
when the object of my love gave himself up to me
without reserve. *Thus did I contaminate friendship
with the impurity of concupiscence and allow the
hellish soot of lewdness to darken its clear sky.* . . .
At last *also* I did lay hold upon love, whereby I longed
to be held. . . ." This *also* (*etiam*) is enlightening,
because it refers to the concubine he took at Carthage and who bore him a son. The passage " friendship contaminated by concupiscence " is then in allusion to male friendship. No matter how revolting
the truth may be, we cannot doubt the testimony
of the culprit who makes a spontaneous confession.

In reviewing this wanton period of his life Augustine regrets that his parents did not oblige him to

marry and thus provide an outlet for his sexual frenzy. It was at this time that his father made his discovery at the Thermæ, a discovery he regarded as a promise of grandchildren at an early date. Monica herself, although she earnestly besought her son to avoid entangling himself with women, was opposed to his marrying, fearing it would interfere with his studies and compromise the brilliant career of which both parents dreamed. Augustine regarded his mother's admonitions merely as the utterances of a simple-minded woman, and he would have been ashamed to allow himself to be swayed thereby. He therefore continued to abandon himself to *concupiscentia carnis*, first at Tagaste and then at Carthage. The crisis was at its height during the period that stretched between his return from Madaura and his reading of Cicero's *Hortensius*—from his sixteenth to his nineteenth year. During all this time, although he continued to study, he was perpetually obsessed by carnal desire and the urge to sexual indulgence.

The love for the drama he had always cherished often led him to the theatre, where, he tells us, " despite the knowledge that all was but a scenic feint, I would participate in the impure revellings of the lovers or, moved to compassion, almost swoon with desire if misfortune overtook them. Yet in either event I found delight." Hoping perhaps to escape from his obsessions or perhaps only to please his mother, he sometimes visited Christian churches, but even there the demon of lust tempted him. " Did I not dare," he cries out to God, " even while the solemnities in Thine honour were being celebrated and within the very walls of Thy church, to desire the deadly fruits of lust and to plan to obtain them? " It was perhaps in church that Augustine first saw and desired the maiden who became his mistress and who was certainly a Christian.

Vanity also had its share in the impurity of his life. " So blind was I in my descent towards the abyss that I was ashamed to appear in the eyes of my contemporaries less shamefully lustful than others; for I heard them perpetually boasting of their infamous actions and I delighted in imitating them, influenced not only by natural lasciviousness but also by my vanity." In his system of theology Augustine may well point to concupiscence as the pivot of Adam's guilt and of our heritage of sin.

His belated desire for marriage, however, was not feigned, and proved that he was not one to remain long a slave to evil living. He honestly longed for a permanent tie, that would oblige him to remain faithful to one woman, even though he could not acknowledge her as his wife. In fact, in 371, when he was seventeen, he took unto himself a maiden of Carthage whose name has never been made known, and with her he lived almost without interruption until 385, when Monica persuaded him to cast her off.

" One woman only, to whom I was faithful, although experience showed me how great is the difference between the bond of legal marriage entered into for the purpose of propagating life, and a contract of illicit love of which children are born that are undesired, but who, once born, command our affection." In the following year—372—this unknown woman bore him a son, that Adeodatus who, with his father, received baptism at the hands of St. Ambrose in 387. Thus Augustine became a father at the early age of eighteen. It was perhaps his affection for his child, and, through him, for her who had borne him, that saved the young man from worse grovelling in the filth of lasciviousness, and even though he was living in a state of concubinage, gave him the illusion of possessing a family and of enjoying family happiness.

However inadequately, the well-springs of Augustine's iniquity were closed, and he was right in naming the innocent fruit of his sinning, the Gift of God.

CHAPTER VI

THE FIRST CONVERSION

IN 371, when Augustine was himself soon to become a father, his father died. Poor Patricius did not have the satisfaction either of seeing the grandchildren he had hoped for or of witnessing his son's success in life. Of his death Augustine speaks only in the *Contra Academicos,* merely alluding to it indirectly in the *Confessions,* wherein, on the other hand, he dwells with such touching eloquence on the passing of his mother and of his " unnamed friend." We may conclude without malice that his grief was by no means overwhelming, and of this we know the reason. Being at the time in the first throes of aphrodisiacal ardour, he probably regarded the event as simply increasing his own liberty of action, especially as consolation followed so speedily.

At the time of his father's death Augustine was already at Carthage, for his friend Romanianus had supplied him with the means of going, at last, to the city of his desire. These means must have been ample, as they enabled the young man not only to maintain himself and pay his masters, but, a year later, to support a woman companion and a child as well.

Here he was then in the turmoil of the luxurious and libertine city that Rome—jealous and deter-

mined—had once hoped to sweep from the face of
the earth. Carthage was the capital of Africa and,
after Rome, one of the most populous cities of the
empire; a place of festivals, of much trafficking, of
many theatres, of religious feasts, and also a seat of
learning. One can picture this lad from Tagaste
suddenly become a city dweller—picture his swarthy
countenance, lightened by the flashing of eager eyes,
as he threads his way along the crowded streets and
beneath the porticoes in that anthill of a city where
are assembled representatives of all the people that
dwell around the Mediterranean. One can picture
him now gazing with awe upon the huge bulk of
the *curia* or the broad stretch of the harbour, now
following with the eyes of desire some Punic damsel
or Egyptian wanton painted and bedizened like an
idol. He soon had his part in this life of the Levant,
which was already rank with the odour of decay, and
he resumed his studies with fresh zeal.

Augustine entered his name at the school of a
certain Democrates, a teacher mentioned only by himself, and began making friends among his new companions. Carthage suffered from an evil affecting
all university towns and that has endured even unto
our own day. Taking advantage of the indulgence
with which youth, especially the bolder and more
irresponsible elements, is ever regarded, the students
held themselves free to commit any excess, and the

wildest among them had formed certain lawless asso-
ciations that partook both of the nature of the
camorra and of actual brigandage. They called themselves *Eversores*, which signifies *demolishers* or *sub-
verters*. Naturally they rendered themselves guilty
of all manner of evil actions, and their favourite
victims were students newly arrived from the provinces—the freshmen, we should call them—whom,
" to feed their cruel gaiety," they delighted in tor-
menting. From the way in which he speaks of them
it is plain that at first Augustine was one of their
victims, later becoming their companion but never
an accomplice. He lived in their midst and confesses that he enjoyed their friendship, but he never
took an active part in their cruel and despicable enter-
prises. In a word, he was a passive accomplice—
one who keeps his own hands clean but smiles in-
dulgently at the victor's bloody fist.

As for his studies the young man certainly applied
himself, for he became more skilful than any of his
companions in the sophisticated art of stringing together words for the purpose of making what is
straight appear crooked. In this he was at the head
of his class and the fact greatly tickled his foolish
vanity. It was precisely at this moment and in consequence of his diligent application to his studies
that he was shaken by what may be termed his first
conversion.

4

Among the works the students of rhetoric were recommended to read were, of course, those of Cicero. Augustine got hold of the *Hortensius,* a dialogue in defence of philosophy which has unfortunately been lost. On reading it he immediately experienced a spiritual change, an alteration of all his inclinations and intentions.

Cicero was neither a great man nor an original philosopher; he did but glean here and there among the Greeks, passing the fruits of his pilferings—to which he readily confessed—through the mill of his own subtle intellect. But he was a lover of all thought and wisdom and had the gift of painting his appreciation in vivid tints. Modernity has spoken overmuch evil of this Roman who suffered death at Formiæ, but for centuries the Western world drew sustenance from his works, and even to-day no one who studies them will regret having done so. Among the various schools he sympathized most strongly with that of the New Academicians. He was, in a word, a mild sceptic, a Latin Carneades, but one who reflected more credit on human thought than did that Greek. He rejected the doctrines of Epicurus without entirely acquiescing in those of the stoics. Call him an eclectic if you will, but he was an eclectic capable of enthusiasms and he was anything but flaccid.

We are not acquainted with the true contents of

the work that influenced Augustine so strongly, for only a few fragments and disconnected passages have come down to us preserved by Nonius and by Augustine himself. Cicero composed the dialogue after the death of his beloved Tullia, and the interlocutors are Q. Lutatius Catullus, L. Licinius Catullus, and Cicero himself. Hortensius the orator delivers an apologia of the art of oratory to the disparagement of philosophy. The others take up the cudgels in defence of philosophy, each arguing according to his favourite system, but all unite in placing the study of divine wisdom infinitely above that of mere eloquence.

Hitherto Augustine had been of Hortensius' way of thinking, considering that the mastery of language was the finest end an intelligent being could pursue. Apuleius had already shown him the existence of something better, but had not succeeded in altering his direction; Cicero now placed before him instead of a fantastic "mysteriosophy" the Hellenic ideal of disinterested contemplation, which makes of man nearly a god. He led Augustine nearer to the Creator, and the harmonious and fervent exhortations of this pagan and half-sceptical advocate inclined him once more towards the Christianity of his childhood.

"This book," so writes Augustine, "altered my state of mind, made me pray to Thee, O Lord, and changed all my purposes and desires. Suddenly the baseness of my own vain hopes was revealed to me; my heart, stirred to incredible fervour, yearned to attain to immortal wisdom, and I did seek to lift myself up and return to Thee." He goes on to say, as a further proof of the change wrought in him, that in the perusal of this dialogue he derived far more pleasure from what was said than from the mode of expression.

A change had certainly been wrought in Augustine's mind. No longer would he whet his tongue, but seek to elevate his spirit; no longer juggle with words for love of gain, but pursue holy truth even at cost of sacrifice; no longer defile himself with illicit pleasures, but once more speak to God in prayer. Had these good resolutions been put into practice Augustine would have been converted at the age of nineteen and by the words of a pagan who died before the advent of Christ! But the cycle of his errors was still incomplete. Before finding himself again through finding God he was destined to acquire a knowledge of evil down to its very roots. If his conversion had taken place at this time Augustine would have become a gifted advocate of Christianity but he would never have attained either to greatness or to sanctity. All ascensions are rebounds from falls, and are in proportion to them.

At the moment, however, he was full of enthusiasm

for the Ciceronian flights. Everything uttered against Hortensius by the three champions of philosophy seemed to have been spoken for his especial benefit, and tended to lessen the spiritual pride of this orator in the making. In this dialogue he found the condemnation of libertinism and of life without a rule of conduct. Cicero showed that to live solely according to one's own will is the extreme of evil; that sensual pleasures alter one's physical aspect, destroy the body, and expose one to danger and disgrace. But above all things Augustine saw revealed in the dialogue a vision of that bliss which is promised to the wise, and henceforth to the end of his days there remained fixed in his mind the fact that a knowledge of truth signifies a knowledge of God, and that only in such knowledge does happiness reside. To be happy—and Augustine desired happiness, nor would he rest until he had found complete and true felicity —one must seek God, must possess God. The famous words at the beginning of the Confessions, " . . . and our heart is restless until it cometh to repose in Thee," had their origin in Cicero's Hortensius.

But where should we find God, that is to say the knowledge that insures bliss? Augustine had learned from the Christians that the Almighty had spoken to man and that His revelations were contained in certain sacred writings which related the theandric epic from the abyss of darkest waters unto the splendours

of the New Jerusalem. So Augustine obtained a
Bible and began to read.

But it was too late! The admirable simplicity of
those pages aroused the unripe but already corrupt
rhetorician in him to rebellion. Compared to the
majestic ring of the Tullian utterances, Biblical
sobriety seemed to him but poverty of language. He
might acquiesce in the eloquent Cicero's condemnation of eloquence, but he sneered at this unadorned
sublimity that to him was both childish and poor.
He was too much inflated with self-esteem and
admired inflation in others too strongly to recognize
in that divine nudity the beauty of the mysteries.
Augustine himself has said that the Scriptures are
entered by a low door, and that to cross its threshold
one must either be a little child or bend low one's
head and shoulders. He was no longer a child, nor
was he as yet a true man; pride, moreover, and pride
in one of its most absurd forms, that of speech, forbade him to bend. Therefore for thirteen years
longer he remained blind. His first conversion had
died at birth.

CHAPTER VII

THE SNARE OF MANI

NEVERTHELESS that same year Augustine did experience a conversion of sorts, but it was a conversion to error. He joined the sect of Mani.

Cicero's fine periods had had one lasting effect—the disillusioned rhetorician was no longer satisfied with rhetoric alone. He was casting about for stronger food, for food more worthy of his appetite; he was searching for truth. He had failed to recognize it in the Holy Books which he had read but superficially, and with the prejudiced mind of the man of letters rather than in the attitude of one in search of spiritual enlightenment. The Catholicism of his mother and of his childhood had never burned brightly within him and, in consequence, had been quickly extinguished by the urge of passion and of knowledge. Probably he now regarded it as the superstitious creed of the ignorant and of simple, trusting women. The wisdom contained in the *Hortensius* was too generic on the one hand and too specific on the other. Those three grave personages who were united in setting philosophy above oratory disagreed when a choice was to be made between the different systems, or when the precise nature of supreme good or the abiding-place of truth was to be established. A decision must be arrived at between five or six schools and between hundreds of different opinions. Among these schools there was one, and precisely the one favoured by Cicero, which declared that man could never be sure of having found truth.

Now at Carthage there were certain mysterious and loquacious individuals who claimed that they possessed and could teach truth—no revealed truth that must be accepted blindly, but a tangible, ponderable truth in whose light all mysteries were dissolved. Like the Christians these men preached a doctrine that had come out of the East, and venerated as their master one who had been put to death.

Mani was born at Mardin, a village of Babylonia, in the year 215. His father, Futak Babak, having been commanded by an angel to abstain from flesh, wine, and women, joined the Moghtasilah community, a sect akin to the Christians of St. John the Baptist, or Mandæans. Among them Mani was brought up, but at the age of thirteen he also was visited by an angel who revealed divine truth to him and, as if this were not enough, in the year 240 he became the recipient of a second and more urgent revelation. Two years later, at the beginning of the reign of Sapor I, he started preaching the new faith. It would appear that the king's brother gave him his support and that at first Sapor himself favoured him; but the sovereign soon returned to Mazdaism, and Mani was sent into exile. He then wandered far and wide throughout Asia, and spread his doctrine in India, Turkestan, Thibet, and China, where Manichæism might be met with as late as the thirteenth century.

After the death of Sapor (272) and of his successor Hormuzd (273) Mani was recalled to Persia by his followers, who promised better days under the new king Bahram I. But they were mistaken, for two years later, in March 275, the prophet was seized, flayed alive, and beheaded. His skin was then stuffed with straw and exposed, hanging on a gibbet, in the royal city of Gondesahpur.

His sect did not die with him, however; he left many writings and disciples, and little by little Manichæism came to infect not Asia alone, but the whole of Europe from Dalmatia to Spain. Less than a century later it was flourishing in Africa, where it ensnared Augustine, who was, perhaps, the most illustrious of its victims, and for nine years it held him fast.

What could the Numidian, thirsting after truth, have seen in this Persian hotch-potch?

Manichæism was the most composite product of all the mythologies, philosophies, heresies, and fancies that had as yet appeared in an era prolific in the composition of religious mosaics and chimeras. To form an idea of this creed one must turn to that jumble known to us as Theosophy. He who is unwilling to

array himself either in the all white or all black garment of the Christian often amuses himself with
piecing together a very harlequin's dress of parti-
coloured remnants.

In Manichæism are to be found elements of Babylonian cosmology, bits of Mazdaism, large slices of
Gnostic speculation (especially that of Marcion and
of Bardesanes), a pinch of Buddhism, crumbs from
the Mandæans, Cainites, and Nicolaitans, and that
main prop of Montanism, the descent of the Paraclete
or Holy Spirit; but instead of entering into Montanus, the Third Person had become incarnate in the
son of Futak Babak. To sum up: this creed was a
contamination of Zoroaster and Christ—an exaggerated Zoroaster and a misrepresented Christ—and
was rendered still more mischievous by trimmings
and condiments borrowed from all the heresies.

The key-stone or dominating idea of Manichæism
is naught other than the ancient principle of the
Avesta and of the *Gnosis*—the eternal, irreconcilable
duality of the " Father of Light " and of Satan, of
Good and Evil, of Light and Darkness. Mani's
dualism was more radical than either the Zoroastrian
or the Gnostic, because it did not acknowledge the
true victory of Light over Darkness or the final victory of the God of Righteousness over the God of
Evil. These two elements, the luminous and the
shadowy, intermingled and combined, are to be found

in all things, both animate and inanimate. For example, even in man there are two spirits, one radiant and the other dark, and the ascetic discipline imposed on the Manichæan Elect had for its object to free the first from the second, so that after death it might enter into the paradise of light.

According to Mani, the "impassible" Jesus, that is to say the man only in appearance (as Marcion pronounced him to be), had appeared on earth to teach the fundamental and irreconcilable difference between the two worlds; but mankind—even Christian mankind—having shown that they failed to understand Him, the Consoler, the Paraclete, in other words Mani himself, had descended to point out the way for the redemption of light from darkness. In his instructions there are the usual precepts of asceticism with a few Indian additions. Man must abstain from flesh, from fermented liquors, from felling trees, from slaying animals, from manual labour, from marriage, from all commerce with women. But these rules applied to the Elect only, and appear to have been frequently disregarded even by them.

The Manichæans had founded a church modelled, even as to orders, on the Christian. At its head was a prince, then came twelve apostles or masters, seventy-two disciples or bishops, called the "Sons of the Intelligence," who ordained priests and deacons. After these came the Elect, who corresponded to the monks, and finally the plebeian throng of *nigôchak,* called in Latin *audentes* or auditors. Augustine was an auditor and an auditor only as long as he remained a Manichæan, although later on his adversaries falsely declared he had been a priest.

The Manichæan Church had baptism without oil and a Mass without wine. Every Sunday the faithful assembled to recite prayers and sing hymns. In March there was a great festival called *Bema* in memory of Mani's martyrdom and in imitation of the Christian Easter. One of the most meritorious of acts was to make copies of the founder's books, and the Manichæans were famous for the elegance of their manuscripts, which were richly illuminated and adorned. Mani himself had set an example here, for we are told he was a clever artist, and had illustrated his own works by means of many beautiful miniatures. He wrote many books: the book of the *Mysteries* set forth the relations between Judaism and Christianity and between soul and body; the book of *Principles* dealt with the dualism of the two divinities; the *Living Gospel* was a life of Christ with a Marcionistic flavour; the *Treasure* treated of the cohabitation in man of the two Principles and of the means of delivering the element of light; *Shapurakan* told of the ultimate destiny of him who does not and of him who does obey the true doctrine; the *Precepts* were an itinerary of salvation; *Farakmatija,* or the

Epistle of the Founder, established the rule of life for the Elect. Nearly all of these works had been translated into Latin, and with many of them, at least, Augustine was familiar. In the year 396 he penned a confutation of the *Epistle of the Founder.*

How did he become a Manichæan? His own testimony enlightens us concerning the conditions that moved him to accept this heterogeneous compound. "Thou art aware, Honoratus," he writes in his *De Utilitate Credendi,* "that for no other reason did we fall amongst these men than that they went about declaring that, having overcome the fear of authority, they would, by means of pure and simple reasoning, guide to God and deliver from all error whosoever should give ear unto them." The first incentive, then, came from pride; the young Augustine would not recognize, even in spiritual matters, the authority of revelation and of the Church, and turned to Manichæism as to deliverance. But this, however strong, was not the sole incentive.

At that time besides being a rationalist Augustine was also a materialist. He was therefore incapable of conceiving of a Pure Spirit, and consequently of the Christian Deity. Now Manichæism was frankly materialistic. According to the Manichæans, not only was darkness material but light as well, composed, indeed, of more delicate matter, but of matter nevertheless. God Himself is made of this light, as are also the stars which are of His Creating (this explains the existence in Manichæism of a species of star worship), and those sparks which are present in our spirit and are ever striving to cast off the bonds of darkness are but sparks from this same light. God then, in Augustine's conception, was a thin and radiant body, and as all bodies sharing in the light are part of God, it follows that he also was a fraction of the Divinity. Thus did the Manichæan doctrine both satisfy his materialism and gratify his pride.

One problem that was troubling Augustine at this time and that would again cause him protracted uneasiness at a later period was that of evil, and it seemed to him that of this problem Manichæism offered a satisfactory solution in that it refrained from making the God of Righteousness the author or accomplice or even a passive spectator of the many ills that beset mankind.

In the *Confessions* Augustine dwells especially upon another argument that then seemed to him of paramount importance—the incongruities and indecencies to be found in the Old Testament. The Manichæans, in fact, accepted the New Testament and the Epistles of Paul (which had doubtless been arranged to suit Marcionistic doctrine), but they rejected the Old Testament, which they declared had been inspired by the adversary of God. But these objections would not have sufficed to bring Augustine into the

Manichæan community had he not been influenced by other and stronger motives.

One such motive Augustine fails to mention, and it was, in all probability, the strongest of all, precisely because he was quite unconscious of its existence and because it could not be reduced to a theory. This son of Patricius and Monica, rent by such violent inner strife, discovered in Manichæism what amounted almost to a justification or rather a reflection of his own dual nature. Manichæan dualism fitted in almost exactly with the Augustinian inner duality. The struggle within him between good and evil, light and darkness, was a daily experience. He was conscious that he possessed two spirits, one which sought to lead him to Divine Wisdom and to God, the other which caused him to wallow in lewdness and commit the sins of vanity. Manichæism, then, was well adapted to his true nature, and on his part Augustine was as a living mirror and proof of the Manichæan dogma. To him, moreover, it meant remission of sin. He could not be held responsible for those instincts of supremacy and of sensuality by which he was often dominated. They were but elements of darkness which the god of evil had assigned to his spirit and which might be held in check but could not be destroyed.

Many years later, when he had really entered into the light, the true and incorporeal light of Christianity, Augustine would call the Manichæans " proud, frenzied, carnal, and loquacious," and would look upon their doctrine as a snare set by the devil himself. But what he terms his " greed of truth " led him to partake of the false nourishment they offered, albeit " without avidity," for he failed to find in it the true flavour of God.   Nevertheless, so thoroughly ensnared was he that he brought offerings to the saints of the sect, " whereas," he says, " had others who were not Manichæans appealed to me even for the wherewithal to appease their hunger, to have given them a mouthful would have seemed to me an act deserving of death."   He also cast ridicule upon the servants and prophets of Christ, as he forcefully confesses in the words: " I did even bay against Thee! "   So fervent was he in the new faith indeed, that he became its devoted apostle, and by his eloquence converted several of his friends, Romanianus, Honoratus, and Alypius among others.

It was at Tagaste that he exercised this apostleship. He had returned there in 374 to teach grammar. It seems he even attempted to convert his mother, but poor Monica was so horrified by the shameful change in her son that she drove him from her door, and for some time Augustine was obliged to live with Romanianus.

Day and night Monica wept for the errors of her child, whom she regarded almost as one dead.   One

night she had a dream wherein she saw herself standing erect upon a wooden ruler, and she saw a youth
of cheerful aspect approach her, who asked the cause
of her grief. Having heard her answer the youth
hastened to reassure her, saying, " Behold! Where
thou now art there is he also! " And turning,
Monica saw Augustine standing beside her on the
same ruler. She told her son of her dream, but he,
sophist that he was, immediately interpreted it to
suit himself. " Mother, thou shalt one day join me
where I now stand." " No, no," cried Monica, " he
did not say I should be where thou art, but that there
where I am thou shouldst be! "

However, at that time neither his mother's dreams
nor her tears could turn him from Manichæan error.
In her determination to save her son at all costs,
Monica appealed to a bishop reputed to be extremely
well grounded in the Scriptures, and implored him to
argue with Augustine and bring him back to the fold.

Who can this prelate have been? At that time
Tagaste was not the seat of a bishopric; the nearest
bishop resided at Madaura, and must still have been
that Antigonus who in 349 had taken part in the
Council of Carthage, where he had protested against
the disloyalty of a certain Optantius. In all probability it was precisely to him that Monica appealed.
Whoever he was he certainly was not an overzealous
apostle, for he met her request with a firm refusal.

5

Augustine declares the bishop was fully aware that he had already successfully routed several opponents in verbal conflict, and he deemed it unwise to risk an encounter with him at this early stage of his fervour in the new faith. Antigonus, moreover, had a most convenient theory of his own in connection with Manichæism which the Christian Augustine could not but condemn. He told Monica that as a young man he himself had belonged to the sect, but that in time and without help from without he had become convinced of its errors, and that in her son's case the same thing would happen. The passive, waiting attitude recommended by the prudent, the all too prudent, bishop did not satisfy Monica, who more than once renewed her appeal, beseeching him to act, and giving way to many violent outbursts of grief. But the bishop maintained his refusal, exclaiming at last in a fit of exasperation: " Enough! Enough! Go thy way! As thou art a living woman, it is not possible that the son of such tears should perish! "

This fine utterance, which became justly celebrated, has saved the prelate from the condemnation he deserved for his cautious lukewarmness, a lukewarmness so cautious that one is tempted to call it by another name. But the " son of tears " was saved nevertheless, and Monica's grieving had its requital and reward in that outburst of grief that marked the moment of Augustine's second birth, in July of the year 386.

CHAPTER VIII

THE BLEEDING SOUL

AT the age of thirteen Aurelius Augustinus had left Tagaste to study literature; he returned at twenty, after his victories at Carthage, to teach rhetoric. He had left as a precocious but timid and obscure adolescent, and he came back almost a man, almost famous, ready for any fray in the field of religious controversy and prepared to compete both on the stage and in the forum. He had set out, still chaste, before the scorching onslaught of puberty, and was come back with a woman who was his wife in all but name, and a son two years old. When he left he had been a Christian, at least in inclination, and he returned a zealous Manichæan eager to make proselytes.

His father was dead; his mother would not have him in her house; everything was changed. But Romanianus—the most prominent citizen in the little town—had taken him into his palace and treated him like a brother, and he also had plenty of pupils, Alypius among others, who was destined nevermore to leave him.

Judging by outward appearances one would have thought Augustine was a happy man. The pleasures of life with a woman, the joys of fatherhood, the consolations of friendship, the devotion of disciples,

the triumphs of apostleship were all his. Thus far
his had been what in our debased modern parlance
we should call a " meteoric career."

As a matter of fact Augustine was enjoying himself. He strove eagerly after wreaths of straw and
courted the applause of approving audiences. He
believed that he held truth in the hollow of his hand,
that truth was set forth in the richly adorned codices
of the Manichæans—and he was enjoying a feast of
celebrity. It was but the celebrity of a small town
indeed, mere local celebrity, but applause, plebeian
and Philistine though it may be, is ever sweet to the
ambitious ears of twenty.

He strode the rostrum and the stage, sometimes to
take part in a stirring drama—epic or tragic, but
always something well suited to display the qualities
of his voice and his powers as an actor—sometimes
to declaim poems of his own, at those public com-
petitions organized by the provincial authorities.
Once indeed he competed for a prize for dramatic
poetry, probably presenting a tragedy of his own.
From his boyhood he had had a passion for the scenic
art, and it is to be regretted that none of the future
saint's compositions have come down to us. To read
only his *Confessions* is to realize that he was a poet
and at times a great poet, but in the exuberance of
his twenty years was he a writer of true poetry or
merely a rhymester scribbling pretentious patchwork?

His school also gave him plenty to do. To those who sought falsehood he, in all honesty, sold the art of succeeding by means of verbosity, and without being deceitful himself, he taught the art of deceiving.

Yet these various occupations were not sufficient—neither all this trafficking in words nor the pursuit of glory—and he needs must develop a passion for astrology as well. He dived deep into the works of the misnamed mathematicians and learnt to draw horoscopes. By exalting the heavenly bodies to the highest place in the hierarchy of beings Manichæism had developed in him a taste for those divinatory jugglings which for so many centuries wore the false mask of science. A celebrated physician, a certain Vindicianus, who once, as pro-consul, had placed upon Augustine's tresses a wreath won by him in a poetic contest, sought to turn him from his infatuation for astral chimeras; but neither the wise consul nor Augustine's devoted friend Nebridius, who was also opposed to astrology, succeeded in influencing him. And so he went on, searching the heavens not for the glory of Him who had created them, but for conjunctions of planets and to read the destinies of babes still at the breast. For when man has lost or has failed to find the true God, yet seeks Him, even unconsciously, his one desire and only consolation is to arrogate to himself some small part of the Divinity.

Augustine, who considered himself a " particle " of God, was striving to lay hold upon the future either by assuring a place for himself in the memory of mankind by fame, or by deciphering the future in the hieroglyphics of the stars.

However, although he was up to the neck in the slough of magic, he would have nothing to do with any other form of witchcraft, and once when a wizard promised him victory in a coming competition if he would consent to certain sacrifices of a necromantic character, he indignantly refused, declaring that were the wreath to be won made of solid gold he would never allow even a fly to be sacrificed on his behalf. Here again, although he does not say so, Manichæan rather than Christian influence is apparent, for among the teachings which Mani took from India was that prohibiting the slaughter of animals.

Augustine did not progress during those two years at Tagaste; rather did he fall back a step or two from the time when he had been moved by the *Hortensius*. The fables of astrology had been added to those of Manichæism; the desires of the flesh had indeed been subdued by his concubinage, but the yearning for fame had increased. These were arid, torrid years, years of poverty masquerading as prosperity. But after this sultry interlude another storm was to break, not one of sensuality, but one of sorrow.

Death, tears, and flight brought these years to a close.

In his native town Augustine had met again one
of the many companions of his childhood, who
quickly came to occupy the first place in his affections, even above Romanianus himself. The two
could not bear to be separated: they were one in
their pleasures, tastes, thoughts, and studies. This
youth also came of a Christian family, but Augustine
with his dominating intellect and his prestige had
beguiled him into accepting the doctrines of Manichæism, and thus the last barrier between them was
removed. This friendship (" the sweetest my life
has known ") had lasted for a year when the young
man fell seriously ill, and one day when he lay unconscious, his family had him baptized. Augustine
scoffed at this administering of the sacrament without
its recipient's consent and knowledge, convinced as he
was that when consciousness should return to him,
his friend would join him in ridiculing the ceremony.
Presently the youth rallied, and Augustine ventured to jest on the subject of this cleansing of an
unconscious soul. He had fully expected his friend
to share his amusement, but in this he was doomed
to disappointment. A grave, cold gaze met his, and
lips blanched by illness warned him that, did he
desire their friendship to continue, he must henceforth refrain from such language. Augustine, greatly
mortified, attributed this change in his faithful com-

panion to the disease by which his mind was still obscured. A few days later, however, the young man died, consumed by a raging fever.

Through this demise death seemed to have struck at everything Augustine cherished. It was as if his very soul had been torn from him and he was conscious of its bleeding. The town of his birth became odious to him, his home a place of suffering; the universe without his lost friend was an empty, hopeless desert. Nowhere could he find solace, neither in the beauty of the woods, in fragrant landscapes, in song, in games, in social reunions nor even in the pleasures of his nights. Everything was odious to him, even light itself. He could find neither peace nor repose, and became an enigma to himself. Why this sadness? he asked of his spirit, but no answer was vouchsafed to him. Conflicting thoughts struggled in his brain; he longed for death, yet hated death that had robbed him of his companion; he was tired of life, yet viewed its ending with horror, for then the memory of what had been would be annihilated.

Tears were his only relief. This youth, who had uttered no words of regret on the death of his father, now seemed unable ever to cease mourning for his beloved friend. Even after a lapse of time he spoke of him in the fervent and despairing terms a romantic lover might use in lamenting over his dead mistress. Never again would he weep thus wildly save for his own sins. Augustine had inherited the gift of tears from his mother. As a child he had wept over the *Æneid*, as an adolescent he had wept for the misfortunes of lovers, and his return to Christ was destined to culminate in a flood of tears. His sensitive nature that was in love with love found relief only in these bitter drops that were his saving—a baptism in anticipation that would render him worthy of the true sacrament.

The tears his mother shed unceasingly over his lost soul failed to move him, to persuade him to change; but now Monica had found an unconscious ally in Augustine's unnamed friend, and he, believing his tears to be all for his dead companion, was, in fact, mourning over his own unhappy soul, mourning for his mother's grief and for life itself, which was being wasted in the pride of eloquence and of fame.

This bitter crisis of pessimism had the effect of opening Augustine's eyes for an instant, and of showing him how, in the absence of love, all those things which have seemed most joyous and rich in our lives become dim and faded. His spirit, ever eager for happiness, could not long bear the pain of this poignant and haunting anguish. He could no longer endure Tagaste, and his one thought was flight. He said nothing of his plans to anyone, not even to his mother; only in Romanianus did he confide, who, while regretting that his friend should again abandon his native town, nevertheless, with his accustomed generosity, supplied the means for migration.

And so, almost clandestinely and still mourning, Augustine fled to Carthage.

CHAPTER IX

THE IGNORANCE OF FAUSTUS

WHEN Augustine wrote his dialogues entitled
Against the Academicians in 386 he gave another
reason for his removal to Carthage, namely his desire
to attain to a nobler profession, to realize greater
fortune in a centre of more importance. But perhaps, as he was addressing Romanianus, who again
on this occasion had shown such generosity, he hesitated to allude to a friend who may well have aroused
some jealousy in the heart of this open-handed patron,
or as he was speaking not to God but to a fellow-
man, he may have felt some delicacy about exposing
his all too human despair.

At Carthage he experienced the relief (how terrible
the thought that it should be so!) that is ever
afforded by the lapse of time; for it is the melancholy
destiny of man that those he has loved best must
die a second time in his inconstant memory! It is
probable that the philosophical studies to which he
again zealously applied himself at Carthage were also
a source of consolation to him. The first problem to
claim his attention was that of beauty, and his first
composition was a treatise on æsthetics.

Augustine, instinctively artistic and by nature a
sensualist, loved all beauty of form or body. " What
else than beauty do we love? " he asks his friends.

"What is beautiful? What is beauty? What is it
that delights and attracts us in the things we love?
Had they not dignity and beauty, in no way would
they affect us." The answers to his own questions
Augustine set forth in the two or three books of an
unimportant work on *The Beautiful and Propriety* of
which he himself no longer possessed a copy at the
time he wrote the *Confessions*. To judge by the few
fragments of it he recalls and chronicles it certainly
cannot have been a miracle of originality, and later
on he expounded far deeper theories on beauty in
his *De Musica* and *De Trinitate*. This early composition dealt with an æstheticism that was wholly
empirical and materialistic and had its roots in Manichæism, and he retained nothing of it save the principle of harmony when he finally came to recognize
the existence and supremacy of spirit.

This little work, however, was the first offspring
of Augustine's intellect (his poems had been but
metrical toyings written for the satisfaction of being
crowned), and a young man of six-and-twenty may
easily persuade himself that he has discovered a new
world when, in reality, he has merely resumed possession of the house of his ancestors. Proud of this
first fruit of his genius, the budding author determined to dedicate it to a man of fame, and his choice
fell upon the orator Hierius, who at that time was
scintillating at Rome, and whose renown had reached

the intellectual circles of Carthage.   Augustine
neither knew him nor was known to him, but he
had conceived a great admiration for this Syrian
who, educated at the Greek school, had nevertheless
succeeded in rivalling the greatest, even in Latin eloquence, and this at the very centre of Latinity.   It
would appear that Augustine sent him his book and
looked forward with impatience to an answer from
the great orator.   But this African Jaufré Rudel
of ours, who had succumbed to the fascinations of
that multiloquacious Syrian Melisande (" as through
fame man may enamoured be "), was denied the
satisfaction of learning how his ingenuous gift had
been received, and this silence certainly struck a
blow at the neo-philosopher's pride, although he tells
us he needed no admirers to make him admire his
own creations.

During this period Augustine read many philosophical works and among others Aristotle's treatise on
the *Categories*.   He had been told this was the *pons
asinorum* of thought, and that the majority of
students, even those personally directed by accomplished teachers who sometimes even drew figures
in the sand, to elucidate the Stagirite's meaning,
failed to grasp any part of it.   Unaided Augustine
tackled this enigmatical and bewildering work, and
found from the first that he was able to understand
it without difficulty.   But it proved less helpful to

him than it might have been, for at that time, blinded
by Mani, he regarded God as a corporate being, and
sought to apply the Aristotelian categories to Him
also, thus debarring himself from the true knowledge
of the Divine.   He also studied music, geometry, the
theory of numbers and astronomy, and astronomy it
was indeed that helped him to the first break in his
Manichæan beliefs.   To the devotees of Mani, the
founder was none other than the Holy Ghost descended to earth, and, consequently, he should have
been infallible.   His writings contained an abun-
dance of information concerning the sun, moon,
planets, and other heavenly bodies; but Augustine's
curiosity having been aroused by his astrological infatuation, he had dipped into the works of Greek
astronomers as well, only to discover that the revelations of the pretended Paraclete were at variance
with the computations of these men of science.
Moreover, after much meditation and reflection, he
came to the conclusion that the Greeks were right
and the Babylonian was wrong.

Augustine still frequented the Manichæan con-
venticles and continued his apostolate, bringing new
members into the fold of that absurd religion, but at
Carthage there was no one who could resolve his
doubts and furnish adequate proof of Mani's infallibility.   He learned, however, that a certain Manichæan bishop would soon be coming to Carthage, a

man famous for his erudition, acquainted with all
the mysteries of this world and the next, one who
would be able to give him complete satisfaction. This
well of knowledge arrived at last, and Augustine im-
patiently awaited the moment when he should be enlightened and reassured.

Faustus of Mileve was also a Numidian, and at first
impressed his eager listener very favourably. He
talked well, much better than anyone Augustine had
ever heard, but he said nothing the young man had
not read or listened to a thousand times before. He
finally succeeded in getting Faustus to himself, and
immediately set before him the nature of the difficulties by which he was beset, namely, the manifest dis-
crepancies between Mani's teachings concerning the
heavens and the conclusions of Greek astronomers.
One has a vision of a young Wagner of an early day,
flinging bewildering and captious questions at this
ancient Faustus who, like his German namesake, believed in the devil and all his powers. But this Numidian, if less learned, was also less arrogant than the
German, and candidly confessed to Augustine that
he knew nothing of such matters, nor did he pretend
to understand them. In fact, after several conversations with him, the troubled professor discovered that
Faustus was nothing more than a propagandist with
a sprinkling of literary culture, and that all his
vaunted wisdom resided in a certain facility of ex-

pression, greater in him than in most of his colleagues. Faustus was aware of his own ignorance, so Augustine tells us. And his frankness seems to have appealed to the latter, for he continued to praise him and to spend much time in his company, discussing literary topics, and reading with him works with which he was unacquainted.

At a later date Faustus was relegated to an island, where he occupied the leisure of his exile in writing a large volume of criticisms of the Old Testament, which work Augustine confuted in all particulars in the year 400. But even then he recognized in Faustus, a man *eloquio suavis, ingenio callidus.*

These manifestations of esteem and of literary deference were of a less disinterested nature than might be supposed. We must not picture Augustine before his conversion as more candid than he really was and as overready to sacrifice his time from purely unselfish motives. It is possible that he had already begun to think of removing to Rome in the hope of a more generous stipend and of wider renown, and he was well aware that Faustus had powerful supporters in that city, where for many years he had been bishop of the Manichæan Church. At this time Augustine was but an ambitious professor, and to prove his ability and culture to Faustus was a sure means of obtaining valuable support. His stay in Rome showed that he had not miscalculated.

So much for the venal side of the matter. As for the spiritual, the avowed incompetence of one of the most highly esteemed leaders of the sect was the beginning of Augustine's repentance, and Faustus, instead of proving a " snare of the devil " to Augustine, was all unconsciously the knife that severed the first strands in the rope that held him bound. He did not at once disassociate himself from Manichæism, for as yet his corrupt and corrupting spirit had been illumined by no higher truth, but the zeal he had once displayed was a thing of the past. He was changed, was indeed still a soldier, but a soldier who was minded to desert.

Those friends were probably Manichæans who persuaded him to leave Carthage and seek in Rome a wider field, richer gain, and broader fame. Perhaps also the thought of Hierius—the unresponsive Hierius—whom Augustine had taken as his model, may have inclined him to listen to this advice; but he was certainly influenced yet more strongly by his detestation of the Carthaginian students. According to his own account this mischievous and lawless company constituted a real calamity for both the professors and the town. They would suddenly invade a class-room other than their own, interrupting the peaceful and orderly course of study, and proceed to turn everything upside down. The famous " Demolishers," who had once been Augustine's ill-tolerated companions, were still indulging in their idiotic, impudent, even criminal exploits, and the unfortunate professor had become thoroughly exasperated. He had never had any liking for them even when circumstances had forced him to associate with them, and now that he was a teacher they offended and disgusted him. He was assured that such shameful customs were unknown in Rome, where discipline was more rigid, and therefore, urged by so many excellent reasons, he determined to betake himself to the capital city, where so many provincial rhetoricians, especially Africans, had achieved amazing success.

His mother was the only obstacle. It would appear that Monica had followed him to Carthage, and on learning of her son's intentions, her tears and lamentations became more profuse than ever. Mani had seized the soul of her Augustine, causing a spiritual separation between them; now the temptations again placed in his way by the Manichæans were about to deprive her of the sight of the very body she had nurtured. Once across the water her son would be more than ever at the mercy of those seducers, and would be lost for all time.

To silence Monica Augustine was forced to resort to deceit. "I lied to my mother, and to such a mother!" But she was not reassured and would not leave his side. One evening she followed him to the port. Augustine succeeded in convincing her that he was going aboard one of the ships only to spend the last hours with a departing friend, and he persuaded her to wait for him in a chapel dedicated to St. Cyprian Martyr, that stood on a hill near the harbour. Here the unconscious victim of his deceit spent the night in tears and prayer.

The wind rose and filled the sails, and the ship bearing Augustine sped away from Africa, from the land to which he was destined to return, after an absence of five years, transformed in spirit and at one with the God to whom his mother had addressed her tearful supplications. At dawn Monica left the chapel to go in search of her son, but she soon realized that she had been deceived, and this cruel treachery on the part of one whom she loved above all others reduced her to the depths of despair. He had left her standing there on the shore, alone with her sorrow, like the Dido of his childhood, following with eyes that doubted their own evidence the vanishing sails of the fleeing Æneas. Like his first hero, Augustine was bound for Rome, and again like him, had not allowed himself to be conquered by the affection of her he was leaving. But the humble widow's tears were not shed in vain as were those of the mythical queen, but were counted by Him who, in permitting Augustine's flight to Italy, was but sending him where Grace would give a new birth to the fugitive.

CHAPTER X

THE CHOICE OF SYMMACHUS

AUGUSTINE arrived in Rome towards the end of the year 383. Doubtless the bearer of letters from Faustus and other African friends, he was hospitably received into the house of a Manichæan, who, like himself, was an auditor. This person probably resided in one of the streets between the Cœlian and Aventine hills, which, as many of the names prove, was the quarter inhabited by the African colony. The Via Capo d'Affrica, which was the ancient *Vicus Capitis Africæ*, still exists.

Officially Manichæism was proscribed. A decree issued by Diocletian in 287 had established the pain of death or terms of murderous labour in the mines for all followers of Mani, and a law enacted by Theodosius in 382 punished most of them with death. Nevertheless, there were still many to be found in the capital itself, and even, we are told, in the Christian Churches, so that at Rome Augustine met and associated not only with auditors but also with some of the Elect.

Hardly had he taken up his quarters in the Manichæan household when he fell ill with a raging fever —probably malaria—that threatened to end his life; but so completely warped was his conscience that he neither thought of nor desired baptism, for which he had so earnestly begged under similar circumstances as a child. But from afar Monica was watching over him. Although he had deceived her and forsaken her, never for a moment did she cease to pray for the salvation of the beloved fugitive. She was unaware of his illness, but she knew his soul was feverish and sore. What will not a mother's heart divine, even across the seas? And indeed in this extremity, Augustine was saved from twofold death by his mother's intercession and tears.

For the time being the flesh alone was saved, but slowly and painfully another cure was being wrought. Augustine continued to mingle with the Manichæans who had offered him hospitality and cared for him in illness, and, living as he did in their midst, he soon discovered that, in many cases, the asceticism of the Elect existed in words rather than in actions. But the idea that sin was something outside his own will, " something that was with me but was not myself," continued to dazzle him because it relieved him of the conviction of sin and of the torment of remorse. All those doctrines that promise man a cowardly tranquillity of conscience in evil-doing are sure of finding acceptance and immense success, for the vile man is grateful to anyone who puts his conscience to sleep.

At Carthage Augustine had attended the polemical conferences of a certain Helpidius who made it his task to combat the Gnostic objections set up against the Old Testament by the Manichæans. The discussions were held in public, and Augustine had noted two circumstances, namely, that the Manichæans used garbled versions of the Scriptures, and that their answers to the Catholic disputants were weak and timid.

No longer a staunch Manichæan nor as yet an enlightened Catholic, Augustine's harassed and divided mind reverted to the philosophers, and again he turned to Cicero, who once before had awakened him from his rhetorical hypnosis. I believe he must have read the *Academicians* while in Rome and, like all who waver, he was strongly tempted by scepticism, at least in that modified form in which it appears in Arcesilaus and in Carneades, and as it is again met with in Cicero's ornate prose. Later on Augustine would perceive that the Academicians held two doctrines, the one exoteric for the general public who merely dabble in philosophy, the other esoteric and reserved for the few. His Roman browsings, however, led him to fix upon the two articles of the first doctrine, namely, that man cannot master truth, and that he who is wise will doubt everything. These problems and others he discussed with his friend and pupil Alypius, who had preceded him to Rome to study jurisprudence, and who was the only person to whom Augustine could open his heart without reserve.

During those months he might have made the acquaintance of Jerome the Dalmatian, who lived not far from him on the Aventine in the house of the famous Marcella, where he was guiding the steps of a group of pious matrons and Christian maidens along the path leading to monastic sanctity. Precisely at that time Jerome was engaged in translating extracts from Origen and the treatise on the Holy Ghost by the blind Didymus, and he was also preparing to revise the Vulgate version of the New Testament. Pope Damasus I had taken Jerome into favour and made him his secretary, but Augustine the Manichæan could not approach either of these great souls. At a later date he would dispute by letter with Jerome, but they never met, or if they did meet it was in the streets of Rome, and neither recognized the other. These two mighty athletes of the Western Church perhaps jostled each other in some narrow Roman lane, but never, either then or afterwards, did they exchange a word.

Having regained his health, Augustine had opened a school of rhetoric and found plenty of pupils, but very soon he discovered that he had escaped from one evil only to be brought face to face with another and perhaps more serious one. At Carthage the students had been hooligans—at Rome they were thieves. They would frequent one master's class, and when the time came to pay, would desert in a body and go to another school. Such an experience greatly exasperated Augustine, who had not yet learned to despise gain, but thought so much of it indeed that he began to hate his thieving pupils and to harbour a lively aversion even to the Rome of his desire.

His Manichæan friends came to his rescue. Precisely during the summer of that year 384 the Prefect of Rome, Quintus Aurelius Symmachus, had been to Milan to present to the imperial court, that is to say to the young Valentinian II and his mother Justina, the petition and reasons set forth by the senate for replacing in the *curia* the altar to Victory which the Emperor Gratian, out of consideration for Christianity, the State religion, had caused to be removed. It was during his stay there, I presume, that the Milanese commissioned Symmachus, who was himself a celebrated man of letters and a patron of all intellectuals, to send them a good professor of rhetoric from Rome. The Manichæans came to know of this, and recommended their African friend to the powerful Symmachus. The Prefect gave the candidate a subject for an oration which Augustine composed and himself delivered. Symmachus, pleased both with the orator and his work, immediately despatched him to Milan.

It was no slight honour for a provincial without celebrity to be chosen by such a judge. Although the Emperor no longer resided there, there dwelt in

ELOQVII SACRI DOCTOR PARISINVS ET INGENS
GEMIGNANIACI FAMA DECVSQVE SOLI
HOC PROPRIO SVMPTV DOMINICVS ILLE SACELLVM
INSIGNEM IVSSIT PINGERE BENOTIVM · M·CCCC·LXV

SAINT AUGUSTINE LEAVES ROME FOR MILAN

From the painting by Benozzo Gozzoli, in the Church of Saint Augustine, San Gimignano

]

Rome a sort of vice-Augustus reduced to the measure of those decadent times, and Aurelius Symmachus was this official. He was an honest man, a good man, and, on occasions, even a kind man. He preached mercy and charity indeed, but he was only too well pleased when the Emperor sent prisoners to Rome to be butchered in the arena, and he was excessively vexed if one of them preferred private and timely suicide to public slaughter for the edification of the mob.

Coming as he did of a wealthy senatorial family, he had filled all the highest offices, which at that time of imperial decentralization had become honorary rather than lucrative. He had been quæstor, prætor, high-priest, pro-consul, and had now been appointed prefect of Rome. In the year 391 we shall find him consul. At the early age of twenty-eight he had been sent to govern Africa, and had perhaps retained a liking for the Punic race which predisposed him in Augustine's favour.

Symmachus was rich and fond of display. When one of his sons was made prætor he spent the equivalent of ten million Italian *lire* on games and feasting. On the other hand he was poor in enthusiasm and imagination, and was consequently a reactionary without breadth of thought, and attached to the customs of antiquity more from æsthetic dilettantism than from austere rationalism. He had failed to

understand Christianity, and while showing himself
ever a loyalist with the Augustus and Cæsar of the
day, he had remained a pagan, and a devout pagan
as well; and although he denied the accusation of
molesting the Christians, it is plain that he was not
hostile to the Manichæans who hindered the progress
of Christianity. It was precisely to this anti-Christian leaning in Symmachus that Augustine owed his
nomination to the post in Milan.

Symmachus derived his fame chiefly from literature. In that desert of dry sticks that pagan culture
was become, the epistles of Symmachus were as highly
esteemed as those of Cicero or Pliny, and his pane-
gyrics appeared as prodigies of style. The poet
Ausonius was his client and admirer; Macrobius
praised him to the skies, as did also his Christian adversaries; even Ambrose himself, who, however, had
replied to his *relatio* concerning the altar of Victory
with much severity of language, and Prudentius, who
for the same reason had composed an entire poem
against him. Both, however, were loud in their
praises of the elegance and purity of his mode of
expression. This laudatory chorus is surprising, for
in all literature it would be difficult to find one who
had fewer things to say and said them more drily
and diffusely. He had neither eyes for the world nor
brains wherewith to understand and judge his own
times. Just as in politics he was a blind conservative,

so in his prose he was the deaf champion of archaism, and he excused his paucity by calling it laconic brevity and his bleakness by calling it patrician sobriety.

Symmachus took pride in entertaining and patronizing the intellectuals, to whatever race they might belong, and Augustine certainly owed the pronounced favour with which Symmachus regarded him rather to his tactful display of familiarity with the classics than to the recommendations of his Manichæan friends. He would not have obtained this favour had he been a Christian, especially at that time when Symmachus was in open conflict with the head of the Italian Catholics—with Ambrose, to whom he was related. What did they talk of in the palace on the Cœlian, this Manichæan who was half a sceptic and this pagan who was also a bigot? Two opposite natures—the African and the Roman, one all fire and eagerness, the other all vanity and ashes; the first destined to become one of the most fervid writers of all time, representing the future; the second, one of the most barren piecers-together of mosaics the centuries have known—a mere parrot chattering of the past.

Poor Symmachus, who was always prating of Rome, of her glories and of the majesty of her gods, was unconsciously patronizing one who, in his *City of God,* would draw up the most precise and pitiless act

of accusal against the rapacity, ferocity, and super-
stition of Rome.   And this young professor, whom
he was despatching in all haste to Milan, even allowing him to travel by the imperial postal service, was
destined, three years later, to be received into the
Christian Church by that same Bishop Ambrose, who
was Symmachus's victorious opponent.

CHAPTER XI

THE SILENCE OF AMBROSE

IT was no recession for Augustine to pass from Rome to Milan. At that time Milan had fewer inhabitants, but was of greater importance than Rome. Not only did one of the two Vicars of the West—the Vicar of Italy—reside there, but there also the imperial court was almost permanently in residence. When Augustine arrived the thirteen-year-old Valentinian II was recently come from Sirmium with his mother Justina, whose favourable attitude towards the Arians had not yet brought her into conflict with the very popular Bishop of Milan. In the course of the preceding months Ambrose, supported by the Emperor, had successfully defeated the eloquence of Symmachus, and people still spoke of the favour in which Gratian had held him and the reverence with which Theodosius had regarded him. In his handling of the question of the statue of Victory he had surpassed even Pope Damasus himself, and Italian Catholics regarded him as their fearless champion. In fact, he was not only the Bishop of Milan, but one of the most powerful men of the Empire, the counsellor, the patron even, of emperors, the most renowned prelate of the West.

On reaching Milan Augustine's first visit was for Ambrose. This was as it should be for reasons both

of courtesy and of expediency, for Ambrose was the
most influential man in Milan. Probably, also, Symmachus, his defeat notwithstanding, had advised an
immediate visit.   Augustine tells us that he was
received with fatherly kindness, and that his affection
for the great bishop dated from that moment; but
the rest of his narrative reveals the fact that the relations between the two men never became cordial and
intimate. The truth is they were never real friends.
In 421 Augustine wrote that he had always venerated
Ambrose as he would a father, but veneration implies
a distance. There can be no doubt as regards the
African's fervent gratitude, but on Ambrose's part
there was always a certain element of reserve that
cannot be called coldness but that yet did not signify
friendship and still less paternal regard. Surviving
as he did until the year 391, Ambrose knew Augustine as a fellow-bishop, and was able to read some of
his most important works; but never once do we find
the African's name traced by the pen of that indefatigable writer of books and epistles, the Bishop of
Milan.   Yet Ambrose was extremely genial and ap-
proachable, nor did his rigid orthodoxy deter him
from lending a helping hand even to pagans if they
were deserving.

What then was the cause of this lack of cordiality
between two saints whom the Church has justly
placed side by side in the first quadrumvirate of her

doctors? By his sermons Ambrose had enlightened Augustine; he praised his mother's piety; he advised him to study Isaiah, and finally, by the waters of baptism, gave him new life in Christ; yet never did he address him at length, solicit his confession, or enquire concerning his doubts. He never invited Augustine to private conference, and left no trace of his satisfaction at having brought into the Church one who was possessed of no mean talents and who was destined to surpass even Ambrose himself in depth of thought and in glory.

I believe that the explanation of Ambrose's reserve, which Augustine's silent advances failed to overcome, resided in the total dissimilarity of their temperaments. Ambrose, of Roman lineage and born at Trèves, possessed a truly senatorial gravity and the placid composure of the North; the African, on the other hand, was all ardour and fire. Ambrose was now a bishop—and a most holy bishop indeed—but before taking orders he had been a man of substance and distinction, a magistrate and a politician, and even now, besides his episcopal duties, he frequently assumed those of *podestà*, minister, or diplomatic agent of the imperial court. But to Augustine, the provincial commoner, purely an intellectual, only the things of the spirit and the impulses of the soul were of importance; he was not interested in the transactions and mysteries of high politics nor even in

practical matters. Ambrose's culture, before he became a bishop, had been mainly juridical and later
theological, and was derived chiefly from the Greek
Fathers. But Augustine's culture was for the most
part literary and almost exclusively Latin. Good
Roman that he was, Ambrose had little regard for
philosophic sophistications, and his own work was
that of the exegete and moralist rather than of the
speculative theologian. Augustine, on the contrary,
was better acquainted with metaphysics than with
the Bible, and was more interested in philosophical
discussions and disputations than in sermons and
morality. In Ambrose there was no taint of gross-
ness. Entering the priesthood at the age of forty or
thereabouts (if, as is probable, he was born in 333)
he had remained a celibate, whereas we know that
from his sixteenth year Augustine had been dominated by the senses, and that almost to the time of
his conversion he found it impossible to live without
a female companion. The celibacy of Ambrose only
aroused Augustine's commiseration.

To these considerations must be added the facts
that Augustine came to Milan recommended by Symmachus, whom Ambrose considered, and with reason,
to be the leader of the pagan diehards, and that his
doubtful reputation as Manichæan and astrologer had
preceded him. This was more than enough to justify
if not diffidence at least reserve on Ambrose's part.

Moreover, a bishop in his position who had to attend to everything himself, think of everything himself, administer a vast diocese, take his seat to-day in the Imperial Consistory and to-morrow rush off to Rome or Aquileia to attend a council, or hurry away to Trèves on an important mission; who must see that the poor, the sick, and the oppressed were cared for, must prepare his Sunday sermons and homilies, write and revise his own essays and comments, fight the heretics and keep the emperors in order, could have but scant leisure for private conversations and interviews.

Augustine paid him frequent visits.   This he could do at will, for Ambrose's house was always open to all, without need of presentation or long waiting in an ante-room.   On these occasions he usually found the prelate surrounded by people come to solicit his aid or to render an account of a thousand different things —when private conversation was of course impossible —or he would be refreshing himself at table, when the young man could not think of depriving him of these few minutes of repose. Sometimes, however, he would find Ambrose alone with a book, reading and meditating in silence. Poor Augustine's mind in those days teemed with questions, and his lips were heavy with words he would fain have uttered, tormented as he was by his Manichæan disillusionments and the temptations of scepticism. But he feared to

7

disturb the bishop, and would wait patiently for him
to raise his eyes, smile and enquire his errand. Ambrose, however, would give no sign that he was aware
of the harassed professor's mute but hopeful presence,
and so Augustine would sit quietly down beside him
and silently contemplate him, finding excuses for
him in his own mind yet always hoping he would at
last speak to him and utter a greeting or an invitation. But time would pass and Ambrose remain absorbed in his book, and finally the disappointed
Augustine, rising with a sigh, would quietly leave
the episcopal palace as hungry as when he had entered
it, and without having received or even ventured
to beg for the charity of a word.

CHAPTER XII

AMBROSE SPEAKS

YET Ambrose, his distant bearing notwithstanding, helped Augustine immensely. It may even be said that, after Monica, he was one of the most powerful instruments of Augustine's conversion. Although the gifted bishop who carried such a load of care and was so greatly in demand did not speak directly to the young man, in his basilica he spoke to all men, spoke often and in lengthy sermons. His great heart, overflowing with Christian and fatherly affection and fortified by Greek culture and his own clear Latin intellect, suggested to him admirable examples, heroic precepts, ingenious applications, and new interpretations, and this rich and stimulating food he set before his hearers with the authority of the master yet in accents of loving solicitude. Ambrose was neither a profound theologian nor a great artist, but he knew how to perform his duty as a bishop—as a guide, protecting and instructing—in a way that has never been surpassed. He honestly believed what he preached, believed with all the strength of his soul and intellect. He loved his flock better than himself, better than his own kin, better than glory, better than emperors and empresses. He was in the service of Christ, of truth, of the one Roman Church and of the poor. He feared neither the wrath of the

mighty nor death itself.   Unlike certain bishops of
our own day, he was not satisfied with producing an
eloquent pastoral homily for the season of Lent and
showing himself to the people only on major festivals,
but himself taught the catechism and preached every
Sunday and often during the week as well, alike to
children and the aged, to the unlettered and the
learned.   He devoted much time to preparing himself for these frequent and lovingly delivered sermons,
meditating on the Bible, on the letters of St. Basil
or of St. Athanasius.   Of the works of Ambrose
which we still possess the greater part is merely a
collection of homilies, taken down by the stenographers, and rearranged and corrected by himself. The
fact that he was a practical administrator and a distinguished statesman did not render him incapable
of rising to conceptions worthy of the mystic. Christ
was ever present to this former governor of
provinces: " In Christ, then, are all things. Christ is
everything to us.   If thou hast wounds to be healed
He is thy *physician*; if fever scorcheth thee, He is
a *fountain*; wouldst thou punish evil-doing, He is
justice; dost thou need help, He is *strength*; dost thou
fear death, He is *life*; dost thou long for heaven, He
is the *way*; dost thou flee from darkness, He is *light*;
dost thou hunger, He is *food*."

And to think that when he was made a bishop in
374 he was not even a priest, had not yet been bap-

tized, and that, as he himself candidly confessed, he was obliged to " teach before he had learned." The voice of a child of Milan (like that of another, destined soon to say to Augustine, " *Tolle et lege* ") acclaimed him for the Milanese pulpit before he himself or anyone else had thought of or foreseen such an appointment.

Such was the man whom every Sunday Augustine went to hear preach in the basilica that was always filled to overflowing with an attentive throng, eager for the words that to them were as strong food. At first our professor paid more attention to the form than to the matter, and was fascinated by Ambrose's smooth and simple eloquence; but presently, becoming ever more enamoured of this form of discourse that did not shine with the light of borrowed splendours, but gushed forth from the fullness of heartfelt *caritas*, he began to pay attention not only to the manner of saying but also to what was said, and to his amazement and relief he discovered that the Manichæans had deceived him even more egregiously than he had imagined. One of the main stumbling-blocks to his acceptance of Catholic truth had been the maliciously derisive comments of the Manichæans on the scandals connected with the patriarchs and kings of the Old Testament. In the midst of all his errors Augustine had preserved a profound reverence for the purity of Jesus—albeit of a Christ incorporate, after the manner of the Gnostics—and he could not understand how these delinquent and corrupt beings of the Old Testament could have been the witnesses, prophets, and images of the true God; so that the Manichæan theory that the history of the Jewish people was but the reflection and work of the god of evil, of Satanas, had afforded him satisfaction.

Now precisely at this time, between the years 383 and 386, Ambrose was composing in the form of public lectures his *Apologia of the Prophet David*, and it is more than probable that Augustine, who was assiduous in his attendance at Ambrose's lessons, heard at least some of these. It was exactly what he needed, for David was one of those most seriously incriminated by Manichæan accusations. How is it possible, they asked, that an adulterer and homicide such as David should be the forerunner, the image, actually the ancestor of Christ?

That which in David is admirable, Christian and holy, Ambrose replied, is precisely his repentance and expiation. God often suffers the best of men to fall that they may rise again greater still, and stand as examples before the herd of ordinary mortals. Many monarchs, indeed, have been adulterers and homicides like David, have been even worse than he, but how many have repented, have bowed the head before the condemning priest; how many have pub-

licly confessed their guilt; how many have inflicted
punishment upon themselves, have done voluntary
penance and wiped out the stain of sin with deeds of
charity?   St. Peter himself sinned, sinned almost
more grievously, because he denied his Master and
his God, yet one word of love sufficed for Jesus to
pardon him.   Then was not the great poet-king
deserving of pardon whose couch was ever wet with
his tears, who ate his bread with ashes and drank
his wine mingled with the tears of remorse? Ambrose
brought this eloquent apology to a close with a comment on the fiftieth Psalm, which enabled him to pass
from moral applications to his favourite figurative
and allegorical glosses, showing by means of the verses
" Purge me with hyssop and I shall be clean: wash
me and I shall be whiter than snow," a prophecy and
prefiguration of the baptism of Christ.

Homilies on David were not all Augustine was to
hear in the two years (385 and 386) during which
he attended Ambrose's courses.   While the noisy
conflict raged which convulsed Milan at that
time and ended in the victory of Ambrose (the Empress Justina demanding imperiously that the
Catholics give over a basilica to the Arian heretics,
the bishop and people successfully withstanding this
demand) he read and commented on the books of
Job and of Jonah. Perhaps even, Augustine may
have been in time to hear some of the lessons in which

Ambrose commented on the Gospel according to
St. Luke, and which began in 385.

Ambrose's chief masters in exegetics had been Philo
and Origen.   He had therefore a predilection for the
allegorical method without, of course, denying the
literal sense of the Scriptures.   Now this method,
which Origen's followers had carried to the point of
exaggeration, making it the sole key to the Bible,
might indeed have its dangers, but it was certainly
at that time the best adapted to remove Augustine's
Manichæan prejudices.   What might in the ordinary
sense appear a stumbling-block and hard to believe,
became transformed, thanks to the allegorical inter-
pretation, into profound metaphysical truth or into
a highly moral lesson.   Augustine was struck by the
fact that Ambrose so frequently repeated the words
of Paul: " The letter killeth but the spirit giveth
life," and by slow degrees he came to see that the
Bible, which he had hitherto despised, was as a land
full of unsuspected wonders to be reached only by
a straight and narrow path.   He discovered that it
was not Catholic doctrine he had despised but a fantastic mixture, the outcome of Manichæan hallucina-
tions and falsifications; and the frankness of the
Christians in acknowledging the presence in the faith
of indemonstrable mysteries seemed to him far
superior to the self-conceit of the followers of Mani,
who boldly promised pure science unhampered by

the yoke of authority and then fed the initiate on
masses of extravagant fables. " I had not yet reached
truth," Augustine says; " but I was already disen-
tangled from error."

Such was the joyous news with which he welcomed
his mother, who arrived at this time. Monica had
not been able to bear the pain of her son's desertion,
and had followed him to Milan with her other son
Navigius. The news certainly delighted her, but
less than Augustine had expected. So fervently had
she prayed for this grace that she was not astonished
at obtaining it; but God had granted only half of
what she prayed for, and she confidently assured
her son that before closing her eyes in death she
would see him a Catholic by her side. Meanwhile,
in Milan, Monica had resumed her daily round of
devotions. She soon came to hang on Ambrose's
lips, and on his part, the bishop made no secret of
the fact that he held the mother in greater esteem
than the son, and if he addressed the son at all, it
was only to praise his mother's piety.

As yet, however, Augustine's mind was not ready
to yield on all points. He still wanted mathematical
proofs. " I wished to be as sure concerning things
invisible as I was that seven and three make ten,"
he wrote, and he had not yet advanced sufficiently to
be able to apprehend the existence of purely spiritual
substances. Such proofs being absent, or rather he

being incapable of perceiving them, he continued
open to the temptations of the scepticism of Carneades, although he would no longer confide the care
of his soul to philosophers who were ignorant of the
very name of Jesus.

Nevertheless, in the midst of all this wavering and
mental conflict, under the influence of Ambrose he
had the strength to form two salutary resolutions.
The first was to give up Manichæism and the second
to take his place as a catechumen in the Catholic
Church.

The way to Grace now stretched, broad and
straight, before him.

CHAPTER XIII

THE DRUNKEN BEGGAR

In Milan Augustine was no longer alone, nor would he ever be alone again. He was born to be a leader and a shepherd. All crept close to him that they might bask and renew their vigour in the warmth that emanated from him. Even as a wanderer he had guided others, and when in sorrow himself, he had given others happiness.

He now had his whole family near him, with the exception of a sister who had remained behind in Africa. There was Monica, there was his brother Navigius, there was the nameless woman who was almost his wife, with Adeodatus who was now thirteen and his father's pupil. His faithful friends Alypius and Nebridius were come also; Romanianus, Augustine's patron, had sent his two sons, Licentius and Trigetius, that they might study under the guidance of his old friend. He had also acquired friends in Milan, especially among the philosophers—Verecondus, himself a professor; Manlius or Mallius Theodorus, a Neo-Platonist who was consul in 399 and was praised by Claudianus; Firminius, who dabbled in rhetoric and astrology; Hermogenes the philosopher; and Zenobius, a *magister memoriæ*—an archivist—who was a devotee of beauty and learning.

Augustine was now over thirty, and there were

times when he felt he had really achieved the worldly
fortunes his parents had foreseen for him and of
which he himself had dreamed.   Yet he was neither
satisfied nor at rest.   This restlessness he thought
might be due to the fact that he was not yet sufficiently wealthy and famous, or that he had no lawful
wife whom he could acknowledge before the world.
Then again he would realize that happiness was not
to be found in those things, or at least, not in those
things alone, and he would torment himself, wrestle
with himself, and be tempted at one moment to fall
upon his knees before Ambrose and place himself
completely in his hands, and at the next determine
to stretch himself at ease on the soft couch of scepticism and no longer waste his time and weary his
spirit with problems which man is mad enough to
propose to himself but not wise enough to solve.
Augustine craved happiness.   He could not bring
himself to accept existence without complete and
assured happiness, and he had never found it in anything.   Neither in the academic and theatrical triumphs of his youth, in his Manichæan apostolate, in
philosophical research, in the embraces of women,
nor in the smile of his child had he found this enduring happiness, this perfect bliss.

Nevertheless, he must of necessity go on teaching,
go on studying, must provide for his family, keep
up useful intercourse with others, and respect the

commands and wishes of those in authority who were
the arbiters of his destiny. For instance, in that
year 385 he was chosen, as the new professor of
rhetoric recommended by Symmachus, to deliver
the annual panegyric on the Emperor. At that time
there were three emperors, Maximus in Gaul, Theodosius the Great in the East, and Valentinian II
in Italy, who was in residence at Milan. It was now
Augustine's task to praise this child-emperor in the
presence not only of the entire court, but also of
his mother, who was the widow of Valentinian the
Great. This boy, barely fourteen years of age, was
emperor only in name and in the insignia he wore,
and even this semblance of power he owed to the eloquence of Ambrose and the protection of Theodosius.
The real ruler was the Empress Justina, an Arian who
had surrounded her son with Arians. The lad was
unfortunate, and was destined to remain so. His
father's soldiers had proclaimed him emperor when
he was but four years of age; in 383 his brother
Gratian had been murdered, and if his fate was not
the same, he had Ambrose to thank for that also.
In 387 we shall find him fleeing from Milan and from
Italy before the sudden onslaught of Maximus. At
the age of one-and-twenty, in 392, he was murdered
at Vienne on the Rhône by a barbarian general. However, in the present year (385), which gave him a
respite between misfortunes, he might have been

living in peace had not his mother, in the desire for
a church for her Arians, brought him into conflict
with Ambrose, probably much to the lad's sorrow,
for he loved the bishop, who reciprocated his affection.

What could Augustine possibly find to praise and
eulogize in this boy clad in purple, hated by one
emperor and tolerated by another, who was but a
timid puppet moving only in obedience to the
maternal wire-pullings?   But he had his orders, and
they were orders that must be obeyed, especially
as, in all probability, they had emanated from the
most illustrious general in Valentinian's service—from
Flavius Bautus, a trans-Rhenish Frank converted to
Christianity, who, although a barbarian and a soldier
(he had been a *magister militum* with Gratian and
had fought the Goths with Theodosius in 381), was
conversant with literature and corresponded with
the famous Symmachus.   For him Augustine must
perforce find some words of praise, and perhaps also
for the Empress Justina.

On a certain day then, in the year 385, Augustine
with a small party of friends and pupils, his heart
beating faster than usual in his anxiety, set out
for the palace to deliver his panegyric.   This anxiety
was not due to any dread of appearing in public,
for from his boyhood he had been in the habit of
declaiming and even improvising, and a professor of

rhetoric, especially when he has had time to prepare his oration, is never at a loss for those groups of similes or those sonorous perorations that impress the simple and elicit loud applause.   But Augustine's conscience had warned him that he was about to utter a series of untruths; that he was being forced to do this; that he was doing it for the sake of applause; and that the very people who would applaud these untruths knew them to be such.   In a word, the whole thing was a farce, and an inglorious farce for him and for all concerned.

Suddenly, in one of Milan's narrow lanes, a beggar stepped in front of him—a man full of wine and indulging in all the joy of his intoxication. Instead of souring the poor creature his wine had enlivened him and he was ready to crack a joke with any passer-by.   Possibly, between one outburst of merriment and another, he may have flung some harmless witticism at Augustine himself.   The orator of the day, decked out in gala robes, looked on this hilarious old soul whose nakedness was barely covered by a patched and ragged cloak, and sighed.   And the sigh was not one of pity but one of envy!

" See how much happier that beggar is than are we ourselves," he said, turning to his companions. " In exhausting study, harassed by ambition and the torment of deep thought, we seek that happiness which he has acquired in full measure and of a quality

such as we shall never possess, and this by means of a
few cups of wine paid for with pence begged from
another. I grant that not even this happiness of his
is pure joy, but that which we pursue through intricate mazes and by strenuous endeavour is more fallacious still. He, indeed, is overflowing with happiness
whereas I am weighed down with anxiety; he is
secure, but I am uneasy. Yet should anyone propose
that I change places with him I should most certainly
refuse, for I prefer to be myself with all the trials
and tribulations that beset me. In refusing I should
perhaps be committing error, for how can I be sure
that I am pursuing the right course? I am his
superior in knowledge? Yet knowledge does not give
me the happiness that wine gives him. And how do
I use this knowledge? Not in instructing men for
their improvement, but to gratify the mighty and
amuse the rabble, to flatter, and to acquire wealth.
At this very moment am I not on my way to act
the part of pander to the crowd?

" You will tell me that one must consider the
source of happiness. That man finds it in wine and
I in the love of glory, and this is considered a nobler
sentiment. But if this beggar's be not true happiness, neither is the glory I seek true glory. Before
dawn he will be rid of his intoxication and will rise
up with a clear head, whereas I lie down drunk with
ambition, and still drunk with ambition do I rise

up. Day after day I am in the grip of a senseless intoxication which affords me not even the slightest exhilaration. Therefore I repeat to you that this besotted old beggar is happier than I. Perhaps he may even be my moral superior, for he earned his wine by wishing good fortune to his benefactor whereas I do but seek to satisfy my own vanity by lying utterances."

Having relieved the carking bitterness of self-condemnation by these and other reflections, he went on his way to the *curia*, there to deliver his panegyric on an emperor who had never done anything at all.

8

CHAPTER XIV

THE PROMISED BRIDEGROOM

AFTER his torrid morning of carnal and spiritual conflict Augustine had now reached what should have been the hour for the *siesta*. Would he rest? There was indeed the temptation to stretch himself at ease on the triclinium of ordinary well-being, but there was also the vastly stronger urge to follow out the itinerary of the passionate pilgrim who would not untie the latchet of his shoe until he had reached the house of peace. During these Milanese years his vacillations were not in his philosophical or religious beliefs alone. Up to this time he had been leading two lives—the one that of the vendor of words whose sale was to bring money and renown, the other that of the intellectual searcher after supreme truth and true happiness. But now the time was come to choose between contemplative ascension and worldly success, between heaven and earth. According to the worldly wise, when one is over thirty it is time to " establish one's position," which means place oneself, compose one's life, settle down. Such advice Augustine had listened to on more than one occasion, and although he did not immediately follow it, nevertheless he was not entirely deaf to it.

It was not merely a choice between Mani and Ambrose or between Carneades and Epicurus, but between the temporal and the spiritual adventure, between the material world and the divine world. In Milan Augustine had acquired powerful friends and patrons to whom he paid court in the well-founded hope of a speedy appointment to the presidency of a tribunal or to some other high and lucrative post. Moreover, he was being urged to take unto himself a lawful wife who would bring him a handsome dower. A magistrate, married and rich—three honourable and desirable estates to which it would not be over-difficult to attain. Had Augustine accepted this threefold and eminently prudent ideal he would probably have become a worthy and useful member of society, and in the end, such is the ossifying action of habit, would have been quite satisfied with himself. But the true Augustine would have died; no one would have remembered that an Augustine had lived; he who we invoke with love and veneration, whom we know as St. Augustine, would never have existed.

Those who are not endowed with even the most rudimentary organ of mysticism hold that religious conversions, especially those of great intellectuals, are due to weariness alone. These hopelessly narrow-visioned beings are not aware that precisely the contrary is the case. They have not the vaguest conception of the pain, fatigue, obstacles, battles, dangers, strife, and efforts that must be made, faced

and overcome in order to lead a Christian life that
is not purely external and devotional. Augustine,
for example, had he founded a family and obtained
the lucrative office he had every reason to hope for,
would have discovered other ways of resting from
his labours than by following the path upon which
he was destined soon to set forth. The remaining
forty years of his life as bishop, apostle, combatant,
philosopher, theologian, and spiritual guide were infinitely more fatiguing than had he spent them as a
trusted official in the imperial service. In preferring
the Church to the tribunal, the conquering of souls
and of heaven to meting out punishment to bodies
and drawing a salary, Augustine was relinquishing a
life of placid ease for one of almost super-
human effort. Fatigue and failure indeed! It
is true that these more strenuous activities of life
in God have compensations that, being supernatural, defy description, and that convert crushing
tasks into feasts of rejoicing. But how make manifest this truth to martyrs to material tasks and to
believers in the modern trinity composed of earth
the mother, calculation the son, and the sacred
machine that is their offspring?

Augustine himself hesitated before definitely relinquishing the tempting ease of the smooth plains
of life. In the first place, what to-day we should
term the " financial question " had to be considered,

the necessity for him to earn money not only for his
own support but also for the maintenance of those
dependent upon him. What property Patricius had
left was small and had probably yielded less than ever
since his death. Moreover, there were four mouths
with a legal right to be fed from this very modest
source of income—Monica, Augustine, Navigius, and
the sister who had remained in Africa. One of the
reasons that had induced Monica to join her teacher
son in Milan, bringing his brother with her, had been
her lack of money. In the dialogue *Against the
Academicians*, which he wrote in 386, Augustine
speaks of " the many needs . . . the comfortless
poverty of those who are of kin to me." Then also,
he must provide for Adeodatus and the woman who
was still his mistress.

Work he must, make the most he could out of his
profession, and avail himself of every opportunity.
He must devote himself to teaching and pay court
to all who could help him to a better position.

Augustine reflected that in order to apply himself
to study both books and leisure were necessary. But
how was he to find time to read and meditate?
Where and how could he obtain books? It is a fine
thing to save the soul, but first the body must be
preserved. It was at this time that he thought of
founding a species of lay community in the company
of his most intimate friends, where, free from all

cares, each should devote his life exclusively to study
and contemplation. This small brotherhood of philosophers would be organized on communistic lines,
each member contributing his entire fortune, the
whole becoming common property. Some of his
friends—Nebridius and Romanianus for example—
were wealthy and sincerely attached to Augustine,
and at one time the proposition appeared really feas-
ible. Augustine discussed his scheme with the faithful
Alypius and Nebridius as well as with Romanianus,
who had come to the north on business and to see
Augustine, who was half kinsman to him and half
client.

Owing to his great generosity and also to the dis-
honesty of certain of his agents, Romanianus was no
longer the rich man he had once been, but the recital
of his friend's difficulties, anxieties, and aspirations
moved him so deeply that he most generously offered
to become the main financial supporter of the community of which Augustine dreamed. Everything
seemed settled at last, and there remained only the
task of finding a fitting dwelling-place for the
brotherhood, when a formidable obstacle suddenly
blocked the way—Woman! Some of the future
members were already married, while others, among
whom was Augustine himself, desired to marry.
Would the wives be willing to accept this life in common, a life of contemplation and isolation? And

even should they do so, would they be able to live together in peace and harmony under one roof? And would that quiet, peace, and concord reign which the monk-philosophers sought?

These considerations carried so much weight that, as the chief dreamer writes, " the dream escaped from our hold, was broken and cast aside." Encouraged by his mother, Augustine began to think of matrimony once more. This was one of the few points whereon Alypius was not in sympathy with his friend; indeed, it was the subject of frequent disputes between them. Alypius had not preserved his chastity, and in early youth had even indulged in passing pleasures, but he was now living a life of perfect purity, and this without any sacrifice on his part, and he was eager to persuade Augustine to follow his example, " especially," he said, " because if thou takest a wife, life in a community and the dedication of thy powers to the search for knowledge, for supreme felicity, will become impossible."

Augustine regarded his friend's lack of passion as unnatural, and strove to convince him that the delights enjoyed with a permanent companion differ widely from those " rapid and furtive pleasures " which Alypius had tasted in years long past, and that we have the example of many who have achieved renown through the pursuit of knowledge, the matrimonial yoke notwithstanding. The paternal heritage and sexual obsessions were not yet dead in Augustine. He honestly confesses that he regarded existence without a female companion as impossible, and that life without carnal pleasures seemed to him no better than a term of punishment. Augustine was made up of sex and a brain, both at white heat and each at war with the other. He would never be saved until sex had been vanquished by the power of the soul.

Only eunuchs, the cold-blooded, Pharisees and Quakers will find the African's sexual propensities incredible or scandalous. One need not be a student of Freud to know that the libido is woven into the basic fabric of our animal life and, in part, of our spiritual life also, from earliest childhood almost to the beginning of old age. Aristotle has said that the two moving factors in man are his needs to eat and to mate. Sophocles rejoiced that he was grown old because, at last, he was free from that fierce and cruel master, sex, and Alexander the Great sadly declared that he held two proofs of his own mortality—his need of sleep and of woman. For this gadfly of prurience stings not only common men but also, and perhaps even more sharply, great natures, so that it seems to be the attribute or burden of genius and sometimes even of sanctity. Strength of blood and of spirit go together. From Dante in whom, according to Boccaccio, "lustfulness held broad sway," we come to Tolstoi, who confessed to Gorki that in his youth he had been indefatigable. St. Anthony's visions and penance and St. Francis's casting of himself among the thorns bear witness to the fact that while the desire for purity was strong within them so also was the instinct they were bound to subdue. Augustine neither pursued women nor was he promiscuous; on the contrary he was strongly inclined towards conjugal fidelity, and for fourteen years lived with one and the same woman. But one woman at least he felt he must have, and so eloquent was he in discoursing of this need and of all the happiness its gratification procured that he ended by impressing the chaste Alypius, who, convinced by this display of enthusiasm, declared his readiness to relinquish celibacy, influenced, however, more by curiosity concerning those delights which his friend and teacher extolled than from any real vocation for matrimony.

Perceiving that Augustine could not live alone, and abhorring his irregular connection as she did, Monica determined to give him a lawful wife. Augustine might have married the woman who had been his companion for so many years, who had borne him a son, and to whom he was most tenderly attached. His grief on parting from her shows that he loved her. Why then did he not give her the standing of a wife? His mother, however, would not hear of this. In the first place Adeodatus' mother was poor, and Augustine with a family to support needed a wife

with *aliqua pecunia,* that is to say, one well dowered.
Moreover, the woman he had taken long ago in Carthage was probably a *liberta,* and consequently not
the equal in birth of this son of the Tagaste magistrate. The Milanese professor who associated with
high officials and with members of the aristocracy
must not contract a lawful union with a woman of
humble birth. It is my opinion that Augustine himself would have overlooked these objections, feeling
himself bound to his mistress by many memories of
carnal satisfaction, and by the affection he bore his
son. But Monica, determined not to yield on this
point, was already seeking a wife for him, and soon
found one who suited all concerned, but who was so
young that two years at least must elapse before the
marriage could take place. As girls could wed at
the early age of fourteen we may assume that the
little fiancée was not more than twelve, and some
twenty years younger than Augustine. It may be
taken for granted that the family of the bride-elect
made the repudiation of the mistress a condition of
the engagement. We do not know by what means,
what tears and entreaties Augustine's consent was
obtained for the banishing of this his first and only
woman companion, to whom he was profoundly
attached by the threefold bond of desire, affection,
and fatherhood.

Here we are faced by one of the problems in

Augustine's life which will never be solved.   Life
with Adeodatus' mother had not always been idyllic
indeed; from the very beginning, he tells us, it was
" seared by the hot iron of jealousy, suspicion, appre-
hension, anger, and strife."   But the fact that for
fourteen years he kept her with him and made her
the companion of his wanderings shows that he could
not live without her or at least that he loved her very
dearly.

Was it a matter of bodily habit or a passion of the
heart?   Perhaps of both together; but this only ren-
ders it more difficult to understand how he was
brought to consent to sending her away.   It was certainly not because of religious scruples.   Although he
was almost a Christian, the woman herself had, in all
probability, been one long before; the vows she took,
which would have been improbable in a pagan, are
sufficient proof of her Christianity.   And who shall
say that her devotion, humble though it was, may
not, in some hidden way, have helped Augustine to
return to Christ?   Nor can she have been guided by
base instincts, her humble birth notwithstanding.   On
the other hand, while seriously contemplating a return
to Christianity, Augustine certainly had no intention
of entering the priesthood, and such illegal unions
were then tolerated not only by the State but by the
Church itself.

He loved her, yet he cast her off; he loved her, yet

without any apparent motive he put her out of his life. If he was convinced that it was impossible to lead an entirely spiritual life with a woman for a companion, then why was he preparing to wed a virgin, why did he procure another concubine after the departure of the first? From whatever angle we may examine them the motives for this separation must ever remain obscure.

This cruel repudiation is perhaps the most objectionable act in the whole career of the first Augustine. Were he sacrificing the mistress to his love for his mother and his desire for moral purity, then we might absolve him; but if it was merely that he had set his heart on a younger, richer woman of nobler birth, then indeed we can find no argument in his defence. What the true reasons for this cruel act really were will ever remain a mystery, but Grace has burnt away even this sin, if it was a sin.

It is beyond doubt that Augustine suffered long and intensely in consequence of this separation. She was forcibly removed, torn from his side, he says, and so deeply embedded in his heart was she that in detaching herself she lacerated it and so wounded it that for a long time it continued to bleed. But not a word does he say of the grief the unhappy woman herself must have experienced, who was forced to leave for all time, not only the man she had loved so long, but also the son whom she had borne in suffering and reared in joy. Augustine gives us but one piece of information concerning her which, while it flatters his own self-esteem, bears witness to the woman's loving and devoted nature. We learn that alone she made her way back to Africa and there pronounced vows of chastity. And so the outcast Carthaginian, driven forth like Hagar, but more wretched than she, for her child was not with her, left Italy in tears, and of her we hear no more.

This break would seem less cruel had Augustine pronounced the same vows and henceforth led a life of chastity or at least waited for the marriage that had been arranged for him. But he did not. His erotic appetite would admit of no fasting nor could he exist without a woman to share his couch, as he candidly confessed to Alypius. In fact, immediately after the departure of Adeodatus' mother, finding himself incapable of controlling his passions, he installed another concubine to help him endure the long wait before his marriage. If the African woman was aware of this, how much more bitter must her return home have been, a return that to her was exile. Did Monica not suffer on discovering how useless her severity had proved towards one who was almost a daughter to her, and on seeing her son once more engulfed in that slough of sensuality whence she had striven so hard to rescue him?

We have nearly reached the end of woman's domination in the life of Augustine. Only for a brief space now will she who ate of the apple, she who robbed Samson of his locks, she who murdered Holofernes, hold his destiny in her hand. Four women figure in his life: two Africans, his mother and his first concubine, and two women of Milan, the second concubine and his promised bride; but of only one of these do we know the name. The others are little more than shadows to us. What, for example, was the fate of the child who was affianced to Augustine, whom he did not marry and of whom he spoke no more? Yet in 387 when he was engaged in writing the *Soliloquies* and the moment of baptism was near at hand, he once more thought of marriage and asked himself whether he should not again love " a fair and modest woman, one who was cultured or who would at least profit readily by instruction and also bring with her a sufficient dower." Are we to see in these words an allusion to that nameless daughter of Milan who had had the honour of being affianced to a future saint?

CHAPTER XV

THE SECOND CONVERSION

THOSE who have told the story of Augustine's conversion (and their name is legion) have pictured it as a series of mansions in each of which the wanderer lingered for a space before his final triumphant arrival beneath the arch of the *domus aurea* of Christ. The story, however, if the rich fund of fact be carefully studied, is far less simple, and if we are to resort to simile we shall do better, especially with regard to the later period, to picture a labyrinth rather than a regular sequence of stopping-places. Restless and ever on the alert, Augustine would knock in quick succession first at one door and then at another. At one moment he would be toiling up a steep hill only presently to find his feet sinking in a quagmire; by night the stars were his guides, but the demons also were not far off. Again he would pursue a path only to be stopped by a ditch he believed had long since been crossed. At times he would draw near to the threshold of righteousness, would listen and peer, be charmed by the sound of singing and dazzled by the light he saw, but never could he make up his mind to mount the last stair. A weight dragged him ever backwards; pride held him fast, and he must begin all over again.

A conversion, unless it be the sudden blinding

light that cast Paul down, resembles the slow convergence of rays at a given point; and until all have reached that point and are all shining in the same direction, the flame will not burst forth. A single solar ray would be of no avail, but grouped together in harmony of purpose the rays will enkindle even the most rebellious souls.

Augustine's spiritual curriculum is, then, less simple than is generally supposed: from the Christianity of his childhood to Manichæism, from Manichæism to scepticism, from scepticism to Neo-Platonism, from Neo-Platonism to Christian Catholicism. In Augustine the crisis was not only philosophical but sentimental, moral, and mystical as well, and the various theories themselves, instead of following each other in orderly succession, dwelt simultaneously within him, ever at war with one another, and each, on being cast out, leaving a root behind that must be dug up lest it put forth fresh shoots.

At the beginning of the year 386 Augustine had still to dig up not a few roots that were barring his way to truth. First of all he must rid himself of positive materialism, this being a remnant of Manichæan doctrine, which declared all things to be corporeal; then he must uproot the scepticism of the New Academicians, a result of Ciceronian influence which had forced him to doubt the possibility of arriving at truth; astrology also he must cast out, which in defiance of Vindicianus's powerful reasoning, he had never wholly relinquished; and last of all there were the temptations of Epicureanism to be overcome, to which his sensual nature strongly inclined him.

There were two problems that tormented him—literally tormented him—more than any others; problems that caused him actual suffering. These concerned the essence of the Divinity and the question of evil. Both, it is easy to perceive, were remnants of Manichæan doctrine which he had repudiated indeed but never entirely abandoned. Ambrose had confuted the objections raised by the Manichæans against the Scriptures, and had brought Augustine to consider Christian doctrine seriously, but he had failed either to make him sense the spirituality of the Almighty or to satisfy him concerning the nature and origin of evil. In his mind Augustine constructed ingenious hypotheses to aid his conception of the substance of the Almighty and His connection with the world, but he escaped from Manichæan materialism only to fall into a sort of semi-pantheism wherein the universe appeared to him as a huge sponge surrounded on all sides by the divine waters and permeated by them. For evil, however, he could find no reasonable explanation, although he no longer identified it with matter and had repudiated the

9

Manichæan conception that made it an " anti-God."
If God is perfect how can He have created imper-
fection? If God is good how can He produce and
permit evil?

While he was tossing painfully upon this bed of
metaphysical thorns he succeeded in definitely rid-
ding himself of his astrological superstitions. He tells
us that he had already practically relinquished them,
but the fact that a friend, a certain Firminus, had
requested him to draw his horoscope, is certainly a
sign that even in Milan it was known that he dabbled
in astrology.   Nor did he refuse to comply with his
friend's request, although he declares he was " *almost*
persuaded of the absurdity and inanity " of these prac-
tices.   However, in the course of conversation with
Firminus he discovered that his birth had taken place
on the same day and at the same hour as that of the
child of a slave in the house of one of his father's
friends who was a fanatic on the subject of astrology.
Now although their horoscopes were identical the
destinies of the two had naturally differed widely,
as must be the case when one party was free, cultured,
and wealthy, and the other but a poor and ignorant
slave.   This coincidence, Augustine tells us, overcame his lingering reluctance to accept the arguments
of Vindicianus and Nebridius, and not only did he
seek to persuade Firminus of the futility of his curiosity, but he thought of other convincing proofs

of the error of astrology, so that he repudiated it definitely and for ever.

Another acquaintance whose name Augustine does not reveal helped him to find a solution to those problems concerning the Almighty and the powers of evil which so greatly troubled him.   As we have seen, at Milan he had made the acquaintance of several philosophers.   One of these, " a huge, inflated balloon of a man," procured for him several works by Neo-Platonists translated into Latin by the famous Marius Victorinus, himself an African, a rhetorician, and a recent convert to Christianity.   These works consisted of parts of the *Enneads* by Plotinus and of certain treatises by his disciple Porphyry, prob- ably the *Return of the Soul to God* and the *Principles of the Theory of the Intelligibles.*

These works were a fresh revelation to Augustine, and so powerfully did they influence his thought that according to some writers he remained at bottom a Neo-Platonist even after baptism.   These authors are mistaken, however, as we shall presently see, but it is a fact that this was the moment of his conversion to Neo-Platonism, which, given the warped condi- tion of his intellect, was a necessary step on his way to final conversion to the Christian absolute.   His previous knowledge of Apuleius had prepared Augus- tine for mystical Platonism, but he was both pleased and astonished to find in Plotinus and Porphyry those same dim enlightenments he had already encountered at the beginning of the Gospel of St. John. The system of Plotinus is one of monistic spiritualism which indeed might well be termed pantheistic, but the ineffable spirituality of the One, whence all things issue and whither all things must return, is declared and demonstrated with a metaphysical vigour which outstrips by thousands of leagues the tangled materialistic mythologies of the Manichæans and the subtle but sterile critical disquisitions of Arcesilaus and Carneades. The majestic Plotinian speculation raised him at last to a higher conception of God . . . of God viewed as a unit, as a pure spirit, as infinite perfection. It showed him the soul of man as a combination of the divine and the material, that is to say, of the perfect and imperfect; it taught him that absolute truth is attainable provided we do not, like the positivists, heed only the experiences of the senses, but concentrate all the powers of our intellect upon inner and spiritual realities, which by bringing us nearer to God, to Whom all things must be reunited, lead us, through meditation and ecstasy, to the very source of the absolute, to that truth which the Academicians believe to be unconquerable.

At the same time the discovery of God as Perfection definitely solved the problem of evil. If all things are created by God Who is Perfection, then all things are good, and evil is not substance, as the Manichæans hold, but merely the absence of what is good.   Not all things, however, are of equal excellence, for, being created, they partake of the nature of the void, therefore tending to change, and at times this change is corruption.   There are indeed discordances and conflicts in the world that have the appearance and the effect of evil, but this evil is derived from a lack of concord in the relations between different things, not from things themselves, which are all—even those accounted evil—in tune with the admirable harmony of the universe.

His intuition of divine light, although as yet imperfect, so exalted Augustine that words of mystical exultation rose to his lips, and the force of the irradiations from this light made him quiver with love and awe and evoked the exclamation: " He that knows truth knows that Light, and he who knows it knows Eternity!   Love knoweth what that Light is! "

In Neo-Platonism, then, he discovered certain truths of Christianity expressed with an efficacy and in language such as he had not found in the Bible, but he failed to find Christ.   The Incarnation and Redemption are absent from the works of Plotinus and Porphyry, who were strongly anti-Christian, and Augustine, notwithstanding his many vagaries and his sensuality, loved and was seeking Jesus, although at that time he was still so ignorant of

Catholic dogma that he regarded Jesus only as a sage, superior to all other men by virtue of the special assistance of the Almighty, but not Himself God. To reach Christ, to attain to full knowledge of the Man-God, Augustine lacked humility. The Neo-Platonists had disabused his mind of certain deep-rooted errors and had led him by the hand nearly into the presence of the true God, but they had also strengthened his pride of spirit. He believed he had climbed to the highest pinnacle of wisdom, whereas " my swollen pride," he says, addressing his God, " did separate me from Thee, and my eyes were closed by the swelling of my face."

The writings of St. Paul, which at this time he began to study with eager diligence, prepared the way for his complete cure. Besides confirmation of the truths he had recently laid hold upon he discovered others which completed and illumined them. At last he saw Christ in His true aspect as the Son of God, of God made Man, and from the Pauline eloquence, which is not rhetorical but quivering with ardent charity and with a devotion that is not servility, he received his first never-to-be-forgotten lessons in humility.

The long road he travelled in the course of a few months was beset with many tribulations; but Augustine already had a foretaste of those delights compared to which all earthly and carnal pleasures are but as " rotting flowers and poisoned viands." In him—and herein we see a sign of coming greatness —the metaphysical processes were neither the calm ruminations of the philosopher nor the superficial dallyings of the indifferent dilettante. Augustine cast himself bodily into the furnace of thought; whatever he touched, even the coldest theories, immediately glowed with heat; he meditated not only with his brain, but with his heart, his very entrails, with all the powers of his spirit; his whole being was engaged in searching, and he suffered and rejoiced in his philosophical victories and defeats as if it were a question not of ideas, but of destiny, of life itself. As in love and friendship he was all ardour, so in his peregrinations in pursuit of truth he became a very flame. Light flows towards light and love responds to love. So passionate was Augustine in his hunger that he deserved to have it satisfied at last by Christ Himself. The final invitations to the feast were about to be issued, and he was now prepared to listen to them—to accept them.

CHAPTER XVI

THE EXAMPLE OF VICTORINUS

At last that battlefield of sin and error that was the soul of Augustine was beginning to clear itself. The hand-to-hand struggle between the Lord and this new Jacob was beginning, and the Almighty, in the forceful language of the vanquished, was already encompassing him on all sides. Earthly doors were closing against him; there was no escape, no rest save in ascending heavenward.

Some particles of the old leaven were still working within him. He knew the truth and desired it, but could not bring himself to live it, to practise it in its entirety.

Not only had the vision of God, thanks to Plotinus, been revealed to him, but through St. Paul he had also been brought to recognize that there is but one Way—Christ. As yet, however, he lacked the strength to pass through the " narrow gate." He had rid himself of the greed of fame and riches, but there still remained one last sinful and apparently irremovable obstacle to overcome—his need of woman. St. Paul, indeed, did not forbid marriage, but he seemed to regard it rather as a concession to the desires of the flesh and to human frailty than as a state worthy of one who would give himself wholly to Christ and to the life of the spirit. Augustine, on the other hand, feared the cares, impediments, and compromises that marriage entails.   After all, he did not need a lawful and hampering wife, but merely a woman for the satisfaction of his desires. He saw, however, that this solution was the worst a Christian could possibly choose or even contemplate, and his indecision delayed his progress towards the final step.   Matrimony was an obstacle in the way of the perfect life and of liberty; concubinage was shameful and immoral; but Christ was still calling him.   What was he to do?

There was no one to whom he could turn for advice at this crisis of indecision.   His Neo-Platonist friends were clever at discussing abstractions, but they could not direct his actions.   It is true they had brought him to the feet of God, but they knew little of Jesus and held Him and His Gospels in contempt. Ambrose was always too much occupied to listen to him, especially at that moment when he was engaged in defending himself against Arian and imperial demands.   Augustine's most intimate friends were his disciples and could not advise one from whom they themselves expected to receive advice.   To whom then should he appeal?

Presently an inspiration came to Augustine that was certainly sent by the Almighty Himself.   He would consult Simplicianus.   Simplicianus was an aged Roman priest whom Ambrose had chosen as his

own instructor and director in Catholic doctrine
when, much against his will and all unprepared as
he was, he had been made bishop. Simplicianus had
lived for many years among the orthodox teachers in
Rome, and was said to have devoted his whole life
to the service of God. Knowing his worth Ambrose,
on his death, appointed him his successor in the
bishopric of Milan.

The principal advocate of the theory that Augustine, converted to Neo-Platonism, remained a Neo-
Platonist until he became a bishop, declares that his
intercourse with Simplicianus was of " very slight
importance "; but as this same doubting person does
not question the veracity of the *Confessions*, his statement is easily disproved by Augustine's own account.
He did not go to the holy man to debate academic-
ally concerning the Gospels or matrimony, but
actually to make a full and regular confession—the
first confession of his Christian life: " *narravi ei cir-
cuitus erroris mei.*" He told the story then of his
moral and mental errors and of his efforts to escape
from them. Simplicianus heard him with fatherly
kindness, and expressed his satisfaction that Augustine had already studied the works of Neo-Platonists,
who came nearer to Christian truth than any of
the other sects. In speaking of these works he alluded
to their Latin translator, and told his visitor a story
that strongly affected the spiritual crisis through

which he was about to pass. It was the story of the famous Marius Victorinus, of whom Simplicianus had been the confidant and whose conversion to Christianity he had witnessed some thirty years earlier in Rome.

His name was familiar to Augustine. Not only had he read Plotinus and Porphyry in Victorinus's translation, but, like himself, Victorinus had been for many years a teacher of rhetoric, first in Africa and then in Rome, and was the author of some works on that art—among others an *Ars Grammatica* and a comment on Cicero's *De Inventione*—which Augustine, conscientious student and book lover, had perhaps perused either at Carthage or here in Rome. Caius Marius Victorinus Afro, to give him all his names, was born in Africa at the close of the third century, and migrated to Rome in search of better fortune under the Emperor Constantius about the year 304, as did Augustine also at a later date. Fortune, indeed, appears to have favoured him, for in the course of a few years he became celebrated as Rome's greatest teacher and orator, so celebrated in fact that during his lifetime his statue was erected either in the Roman Forum or in the Forum of Trajan, we know not which. This was an unusual honour even in those degenerate days, for anyone who was neither a Cæsar nor a general. At that time Victorinus was a declared pagan, and it would appear that he, like so many of his contemporaries, had received initiation in the Egyptian mysteries. It followed that he abhorred Christianity, and even in his works on rhetoric found means of casting malicious slurs on the virginity of Mary and on the Resurrection of Christ. Someone must have pointed out to him, however, that not by mere witticisms could a religion be stamped out that had already conquered half the empire and the emperors themselves, and it was precisely with the intention of combating Christianity with philosophical weapons (among other works he had translated Aristotle's *Categories* and the *Isagoge* by Porphyry) that he undertook a careful study of the Bible. But as has happened in so many cases, the result differed widely from what he had expected. He had gone deeply into the Scriptures for the purpose of demolishing them, but instead their study drove from his spirit that pagan mythology and those " mysteriosophies " to which he had once been attached. Let it be borne in mind that he was no uncultured and impressionable youth at this time, but a man well over fifty, at the zenith of his fame and experience, and that all his friends, admirers, and patrons were pagans.

Victorinus confided the fact of the astounding change he had undergone to Simplicianus. " Thou must know that I am now a Christian! " " Never will I believe this until I have seen thee in Christ's

Church," said the wise priest.   "Do walls make the Christian, then?" laughed Victorinus.

But the astute controversialist himself could not long rest content with this answer, which smacked of the sophist.   The Church does not consist of walls only, but is the acknowledgment of one's brotherhood with all who have been redeemed by Christ; it is the public profession of one's inward beliefs.   But the famous teacher feared the ridicule of his friends, or worse still, that they might become his enemies.   Grace had already descended upon him, however, and his eyes were soon opened to his own cowardice.   He had never blushed when serving the spirits of evil; should he now blush to serve Christ?   At last one day he said to Simplicianus: "Let us go to the Church, for I wish to become a Christian," and as soon as he had mastered the rudiments of the doctrine he entered his name among the candidates for baptism on the night before Easter.   The sensation this conversion produced in Rome was enormous; the Christians rejoiced while the pagans loudly voiced their amazement.   At that time it was the custom for the candidates for baptism to pronounce a formula or profession of faith from some prominent place in the basilica and in the presence of the people. However, in consideration of the delicate position in which Victorinus found himself, the priests offered to allow him to make his profession behind closed doors; but the former orator refused, saying: " I have spoken so many false and futile words in public! Shall I now hide myself in acknowledging Truth? " And in a loud voice he declared his conversion to the new faith in the presence of an admiring and deeply affected multitude.

Henceforth all his talents were devoted to explaining and defending that Christianity he had once sought to destroy. He was the author of commentaries on several of St. Paul's Epistles, wrote in confutation of the Arian heresy, and even launched into verse to sing the mystery of the Trinity in three beautiful hymns. Like Augustine he also had been led to the light of Christianity by the glimmerings of Neo-Platonism, and at heart he remained ever somewhat of a Platonist, so that St. Jerome held his theology in but slight esteem. He was, in a word, the Marsilio Ficino of his era, who honestly believed in the possibility, the desirability even, of a union between the Christian dogma and the Platonic philosophisms, an opinion which is not without foundation, for even in our own times certain devout Catholics have regarded Plato almost as a precursor of Christ; nor can it be denied that the Gospel of John, for example, as well as the writings of the Areopagite, do contain somewhat both of Platonism and of Neo-Platonism. In the *City of God* Augustine relates how, according to Simplicianus's account, a Platonist had once expressed the wish that the opening words of St. John's Gospel might be displayed in letters of gold in the most prominent place in every church. That Platonist can have been none other than Victorinus.

No matter what opinion may prevail concerning the impeccability of Victorinus's theology, the fact remains that he lived a faithful soldier of the Church, and he proved his steadfastness when, in the year 362, Julian the Apostate having issued an edict forbidding Christians to teach literature and rhetoric, he chose rather to close his flourishing and very lucrative school than to deny his faith.

The story of this conversion impressed Augustine so deeply that he confessed he was " aflame with the desire to imitate Victorinus." The many points of similarity between the two men enhanced the impression. Both were Africans, both teachers of rhetoric, both avid of fame, both had been led to Christianity by the Neo-Platonic writings. On Augustine's side the final act, that of complete conversion and of baptism, was still in abeyance. The desire was there, but his mind was not yet resolved.

In Augustine the struggle between his two original natures, his two conflicting wills, was still fierce. One—the carnal nature—was old, the other—the spiritual nature—was of new birth. He had as yet been unable to unite them and thus attain to peace. He still lived in both, but now more strongly in the

spiritual. Only the dragging chain of habit withheld him from slaying the old man within him and
rising again—his spirit at peace—in the new man.
Libido it still was that chained him down; " for," as
he himself subtly observes, " it is the perversion of the
will that creates *libido*; submission to *libido* creates
habit, and non-resistance to habit creates the necessity." He compares himself to a man still half asleep
who, although aware how much better is waking
than sleeping, and how necessary it is that he should
rouse himself, yet deliberately prolongs his drowsy
state, yielding to the desire of losing himself once
more in unconsciousness.

The example of Victorinus had given the dozing
Augustine a first vigorous shake. One more and he
would open his eyes—eyes dimmed by tears indeed—
to the dawning light of Christ.

CHAPTER XVII

THE EXAMPLE OF ANTHONY

No one, not even his two most faithful companions Alypius and Nebridius, did Augustine take fully into his confidence. Younger than he, but far less passionate and complex, they would have been incapable of following the intricacies of his thought processes and all the sudden veerings of sentiment which so greatly agitated him. As a consequence he suffered far more acutely than those around him suspected. Only his mother, perhaps, could see further into the depths of her son's painful emotions; she who had made him in her own image and was guided not only by that superior intuition peculiar to her sex, but by her great love and a rapidly growing hope as well. Augustine's spirit was like a March day, when winter with its rigours is about to depart, and spring has not yet decided to set Nature free with her all-conquering smile; when on one and the same day we may have the mists of October, the sunshine of May, the gales of January, and the rains of November, and already along the banks and in the naked hedge-rows a few violets, half hidden by their wet leaves, push up their purple heads from beneath their hoods of green.

It happened, then, that on a certain day in July, Augustine received a visit from a court dignitary

whose name was Pontitianus, and who like himself
was an African. Pontitianus found him alone with
Alypius, for Nebridius was gone to help Verecondus,
a teacher of grammar and one of Augustine's friends.
Augustine's house was sufficiently luxurious in its
appointments and boasted even a gaming-table; but
instead of dice Pontitianus saw a book lying on this
table which he was curious enough to examine. The
volume contained the Epistles of Paul, which, as we
know, Augustine was then studying for the purpose
of refining the fruits of his Neo-Platonic initiation
in the fire of the apostolic word.

Pontitianus, who was a devout Christian, was delighted by this discovery; he had believed the volume
to be one of those text-books which teachers of rhetoric use in lecturing, and instead he had come upon
the most brilliant letters ever penned by man—the
fifth gospel, for the conquering of the Gentiles.
Augustine told Pontitianus of his admiration for the
Pauline writings, and the visitor soon brought
the conversation round to the life and works of
Anthony the Great, the anchorite of Egypt who had
died in 356, two years after the Numidian's birth.
Augustine, to whom the names of even the most
obscure of Roman rhetoricians were familiar, had
never heard of this famous patriarch of monasticism.
Yet Athanasius had written his story within a year
of his death; but probably Evagrius had not yet

translated this biography into Latin, and Augustine still found Greek difficult to read. He learned then from Pontitianus that Anthony, born at Coma in 251 of wealthy parents, becoming an orphan at the age of twenty, had given all he possessed to the poor, placed his only sister in a " refuge for virgins," and had gone forth alone to lead a life of penance at no great distance from the city and the house of his birth. Presently, however, finding that proximity to the city hindered him in his purpose of weaning himself from all worldly interests and earthly affections, he went farther into the desert and took up his abode on a wooded slope of Mount Pispin. Pontitianus told how for at least ten years Anthony warred continuously against the temptations of the flesh, which, in this young African, were manifold and violent.

" The enemy," Cavalca wrote at a later date, " would fire his blood . . . and at night cause the most beautiful and voluptuous females to appear to him; but he, mindful of the fires of hell and of the bed of worms prepared for the impure, would stoutly resist them and argue with them, and by making mock of the enemy, would conquer him." These temptations left him no peace either sleeping, waking, praying, or resting, yet he always succeeded in withstanding them. He slept upon a rough mat or upon the bare ground, lived only on bread and water, and would fast for as many as four days at a time. Later on, to avoid his numerous visitors and those who came to him for advice or healing, he withdrew to a still more remote region, and for many years dwelt alone in the Thebaid with a store of biscuits as hard as rocks that was replenished every six months. At the time of Diocletian's persecution Anthony, braving martyrdom, went boldly to Alexandria to comfort the Christians, and he again visited that city in 338 to support the great Athanasius against the Arians. But his narrow cell, although hidden away so far, remained ever the goal of pilgrimages from all parts of the East, until death took Anthony at the age of one hundred and five.

The story of this heroic anchorite who had spent more than seventy years in the desert in hand-to-hand strife with demons, and who had remained ever victorious, was an unexpected revelation to Augustine. In a sense Anthony was his very opposite, for he had received no education, had been familiar with no language other than Coptic, and had held literature and philosophy in contempt. Once when a certain learned man went to see him and asked how he could endure such solitude without books, he replied: "My book is Nature in all these things God has created. When I so desire it Nature unaided can open for my perusal the works of the Omnipotent." Augustine, devoted to literature and to the end of

his days a lover and producer of books, did not resemble him in this respect, but in common with
Anthony he was the victim of two powerful stimu-
lants to sin—the temptations of the flesh and of
pride. But if Anthony, a man like himself, like himself an African, had overcome these temptations, why
should not he do so also?

Pontitianus went on to tell him that the monastic
life was neither impossible nor rare, and that a convent for virgins founded by Ambrose actually existed
in Milan itself. But in Egypt and Palestine, he assured
Augustine, the followers of Anthony and of Paul of
Thebes were so numerous that colonies of monks,
called " *lauras*," had been established under the guidance of Pachomius, while innumerable hermits dwelt
in caves or huts far from the habitations of men. The
example of Anthony was also influencing many who
lived in the midst of worldly splendours and held
exalted posts under Government. Pontitianus further
related that once, years before at Trèves, while the
Emperor was enjoying the games in the arena, he
with three companions, who were all court digni-
taries, went for a walk in certain gardens outside the
city walls, and two members of the party, wandering
farther afield, came upon a hovel where dwelt some
monks. While resting there the friends perused a
life of Anthony which they found at hand, and one
of them was so strongly affected by it that he then

and there decided to become a hermit and persuaded his companion to follow his example. When, after a long search, Pontitianus and the friend who was with him finally discovered them in that remote spot, they firmly declared their intention of renouncing the world and their resolve to remain where they were at all costs. Although he envied them Pontitianus himself had not had the courage to follow their example, but the better to demonstrate the power of this sudden conversion he related some particulars which greatly increased Augustine's astonishment. He said that not only were both men held in high esteem by the Emperor and soon to be promoted to positions of still greater importance, but both also were about to be married, and when the women to whom they were betrothed learned how holy was the motive which had caused them to be abandoned, they entered a convent for virgins.

Pontitianus told his story with much fervour. When he had finished he attended to the errand on which he was come in the first place, and then took his departure. Augustine, overwhelmed by a confused flood of thoughts and shame, was left alone with Alypius.

CHAPTER XVIII

THE CHILD'S COMMAND

ALL unconsciously the honest Pontitianus had urged Augustine to the extreme brink beyond which, if he would save himself, he must of necessity soar to the heights.

The words he had listened to had stripped him of the last faded rags that had concealed his wretched condition; he stood naked—stark naked—in his own sight. He saw himself as he was, " ugly, filthy, deformed, bruised and covered with sores," and he loathed himself, but could not flee from himself; he hated himself, but lacked the courage to change. Twelve years had elapsed since he had first looked upon the august face of wisdom in the pages of the *Hortensius,* but instead of raising himself to its level and soaring thence to Divine Truth he had become entangled in the nets spread by Mani, and had allowed the power of his will to be sapped in the arms of women. In former days he might have soothed his conscience with the reflection that he could not be sure of really possessing Truth, but now his spirit was convinced. " Mani is an impostor. The Almighty calls me. Jesus is the only way and Paul is my guide." Augustine's intellectual conversion had been complete before that hour; he believed what the Christians taught, wished to be a Christian, was a

Christian in desire and thought. His acceptance of
Christ dated from the moment when Paul's faith had
transfixed and conquered him.

What then remained to be accomplished? He must
live the Christian life, introduce the faith he now
acknowledged into his daily life, renounce those
voluptuous habits that still held him prisoner, follow
Anthony's example in subduing the flesh and eman-
cipating himself from slavery to women. The battle
that raged in Augustine's breast was not between
truth and error, God and Satan, faith and doubt,
but between chastity and lust, the desire for perfect
purity and the longing for sensual ecstasy, between
the spirit and sex.

This was why, as Pontitianus told of Anthony, the
conqueror of impurity, Augustine was scorched and
torn by shame. So long as his complete conversion
had been delayed by conflicting theories or by differ-
ences between one faith and another, Augustine had
suffered indeed, but not as he now suffered when opposition to that conversion no longer derived from
the lofty regions of the intellect but was the result
of hot blood, of lust until now insatiable.

This and this only was the nature of the " great
inner struggle " that convulsed and humiliated his
warring spirit, and hardly had Pontitianus taken his
departure when Augustine cast himself upon Alypius's breast, the distortions of his countenance be-

traying the violence of his spiritual conflict. "What ails us?" he cried. "Didst thou not hear? The unlearned arise and take heaven by force, while we, with all our learning, wallow in lust and blood! We are ashamed to follow them, and yet ashamed of our inability so to do!"

Alypius heard him in mute astonishment, seeing him so different from his usual self, his damp brow, flaming cheeks, flashing eyes, and hoarse voice betraying his state of exaltation even more clearly than did his words themselves. Without waiting for his friend to speak Augustine left him and hastened into the garden, trusting to solitude to calm this delirium. Alypius followed him, however, and together they strode away from the house to the foot of the garden, where they seated themselves side by side. But Augustine's rage against himself would not be appeased. One seeing him at this moment might well have pronounced him a gesticulating maniac in the clutches of an evil vision. Now he would tear his hair or smite his brow, now wave in the air the thin volume of Epistles he had brought with him or clasp his knees with tightly locked fingers, sighing and trembling but uttering no word. He was enraged with himself, horrified by the relentless malady that afflicted his spirit, accusing himself harshly of being too great a coward to break the chains that held him down. He was eager enough to burst them asunder though it be at cost of lacerating his flesh, but even now evil visions and memories of past lustfulness would assail him, and he feared to attempt a reformation lest he find a life of chastity impossible. " I will put an end to it all," he told himself, and marvelled that the spirit which controls so many parts of the body could not control itself, and that having acquired certainty at last, it was unable to overcome the shameful passion that held it in bondage. In his mind's eye he beheld those (and they are legion) who have pronounced vows of chastity, and he saw that they were happy, and consoled by such joys as no carnal indulgence can procure. How then could any man, for a single fleeting spasm of enjoyment, relinquish those never-ending spiritual raptures, the serene bliss of contemplation, the eternal friendship of Christ?

Such then was the silent but fierce conflict that was raging in Augustine's breast between the old ego and the new. And when, having subjected himself to pitiless introspection, he had gathered together and heaped up before his inner vision the great mass of his own wretchedness, so overwhelming was the loathing that assailed him that a flood of tears dimmed his sight. Wishing to abandon himself freely and in solitude to the relief of this new crisis, he left Alypius, who sat still lost in deep astonishment, and withdrawing to a distance cast himself down at the foot of a spreading fig-tree. Immediately the hot and bitter tears overflowed and bathed his face, and his suffering spirit that had been so storm-swept and frenzied was refreshed by that redeeming flood, and found itself again at last.

The sunset hour was near at hand; the heat of midsummer weighed upon the wall-encompassed garden, and no breeze stirred the fig-tree's broad, rough leaves. Centuries before, in far distant India, another fig-tree had witnessed the enlightening and awakening of Prince Siddhartha who became the Buddha, and it was beneath a fig-tree in Palestine that the far-seeing eye of Jesus had perceived and drawn to Himself one of the Apostles, the reluctant Nathaniel.

Augustine was ignorant of these events or perhaps did not recall them, but amidst sobs and tears he lifted up his voice, crying out to the living God: " How long, O Lord, how long shall Thy wrath endure against me? "

Yet that too fondly cherished sin of earthly passion still held him back and caused him to falter on the brink. Again he cried: " When shall I achieve salvation? When cast off my fetters? To-morrow, perhaps? Or the day after? Shall I always say to-morrow, and will to-day never dawn for me? Why not this very hour? Why not end it at once, now and for ever? "

Suddenly, while the flood of grief still surged upwards from his tortured heart, he became aware of the voice of a child, boy or girl he knew not which, speaking in a neighbouring house.

"Take up and read," said the sweet young voice. "Take up and read."

As he listened, seeking to remember if those words were part of some childish game and deciding they were not, Augustine's expression changed. The voice of this child of Milan heard at that precise moment could be none other than the voice of God. Starting to his feet Augustine forced back his tears and hastened to the spot where he and Alypius had sat and where he had left the little volume of Paul's Epistles. He had remembered what Pontitianus had told him of Anthony, how one day on hearing a verse from the Bible, he had been moved to alter his way of life completely and unhesitatingly. Augustine seized the book, and, opening it at random, the first words that met his tear-dimmed eyes were these from the Epistle to the Romans: "Not in rioting and drunkenness, not in chambering and wantonness, not in strife and envying; but put ye on the Lord Jesus Christ and make not provision for the flesh."

He read no further. That brief verse, so miraculously adapted to his own case, was all he needed. At once a steady light that dispelled all shadows of doubt suffused and comforted his spirit. This was the end! This was victory! That moment marked the anni-

SAINT AUGUSTINE'S CONVERSION

From the painting by Benozzo Gozzoli, in the Church of Saint Augustine, San Gimignano

hilation of those carnal passions which for sixteen years had possessed Augustine and had appeared invincible. The last obstacle was overcome; woman as a sex mate was banished and repudiated. He was released, he could breathe freely; nothing now separated him from Christ.

With his finger between the pages of the book to mark the redeeming passage, he poured out his story to Alypius, dwelling on the long struggle to reach this supreme moment, and on the enemy's final defeat. Alypius took the book from him that he might read Paul's words for himself, and farther on he came to these other words: " Him that is weak in faith, receive."

" This passage," said Alypius, " is meant for me."

Chaste as he was by both nature and inclination, Alypius vowed to follow and help his friend and master on the way he had now definitely chosen. Having been his companion in error he now promised himself he would bear him company in his ascent towards Truth, a promise by which he stood until the end.

In their eagerness to share with her the joy of their own happiness the two friends hastened to Monica and told her all. The saintly widow, who had paid the price of her son's tears with so many of her own, now wept afresh, but the tears of that hour were of triumph and rejoicing. The dream was come true.

Her son stood beside her at last on the same " rule of faith," and she praised the Lord Who, after much suffering, had granted her this boon. Augustine protested to his mother that henceforth he would renounce all earthly and carnal bonds. For him, and for them all, a new life was beginning. The child's command had been obeyed and God's decrees should be honoured until the end. Flesh was conquered and the spirit was free to become the willing slave of Christ. No more tears—the time of rejoicing was at hand. Augustine's brain had long been Christian; now his heart was Christian also, and Christian should his life be in its every phase.

CHAPTER XIX

DETACHMENTS

The majority of critics are of opinion that the crisis of tears in the garden marked the moment of Augustine's passage to Christianity, while a few—a very few—suggest that for a considerable period after the year 386 he still remained a Neo-Platonist.

Both suppositions are mistaken. His real conversion took place neither in July 386 nor still less afterwards, but actually at a much earlier date and only a few months after his arrival in Milan. The reader who has carefully followed the ascending spiral of Augustine's mental processes, which, its windings and twistings notwithstanding, was steadily mounting towards a given point, must have perceived that the crisis induced by the words of Pontitianus was but the dramatic corollary of a resolution already taken and of a truth already acknowledged—the tearing away, at cost of much bleeding, of the last scab on a shameful sore. It was not of error that Augustine rid himself on that day but of erotic enchantment.

When he arrived in Milan his faith in Manichæism had already been shaken by his disappointment in Faustus and by his Roman experiences. Ambrose carried on the work of liberation by revealing to him the beauty, profundity, and infallibility of the Bible;

Plotinus and Porphyry delivered him from the last traces of Manichæan materialism and academic scepticism, and supplied him with a satisfactory solution of the problem of evil; and finally St. Paul taught him humility of spirit, the identity of the *Unigenitus* with the Platonic *Light,* and the absolute necessity of rebirth in Christ. When he went to the priest Simplicianus with the intention of confessing, of acquainting him with the tangle and the disentangling of his errors, Augustine was already a Christian and desirous of a life in Christ; over his intellect faith already held full sway, although as yet his way of life was unaffected by it. The very fact that he confessed to a Catholic priest and sought his advice in his endeavours to free himself from the bonds of concupiscence clearly demonstrates that he already recognized the legitimacy and sovereignty of the Roman Church, and intended to subject his line of conduct to its dictates. If the example of Victorinus had stirred him deeply, arousing in him the desire to follow it, this was because his heart was already prepared for such a step; and had his opinions been unChristian or anti-Christian the mere story of a conversion would not have sufficed to convert him. He had known so many conversions already! Nor was Augustine of an apish nature; passionate he was indeed, but also a subtle reasoner who must comprehend before he could believe.

The scene in the Milanese garden therefore is not comparable, as many believe it to be, with that which took place on the road to Damascus some three hundred and fifty years earlier. Augustine's conversion was not a sudden shining forth and flooding of light in a blind heart. It had been a slow and gradual process, and was the result rather of much testing and intellectual research than of a sudden outburst. From the time when, still a child, he had pleaded for baptism, until it caused the supreme spark to descend upon him, Grace had always assisted him. On that July day Augustine did not pass suddenly from unbelief to faith; he did but register his resolve henceforth to apply the rule of faith to the practical contingencies of life. This was indeed a most important and decisive event, but one in itself more ethical than mystical.

He must now fulfil this resolve and alter his course without repining. God, Augustine tells us, had drained his heart of every drop of impurity and thus liberated him from the threefold lust which had so long held him irresolute, on the shore of the divine ocean—the lust of fame, of gain, and of the flesh. The two wills had vanished at last; one alone remained, that desired only what God willed. Never would Augustine turn back during the four-and-forty years he had still to live, and if he ever retraced in memory the course of his errors, it was but to

weep over the sins of his dead ego and to raise his
voice in a hymn of thanksgiving to his Liberator.

The first renunciation Augustine determined upon
was that of his chair of dialectics. He would no
longer sell himself, nor sell to youth those words
and arts which served almost invariably to express
evil passions or were used in their defence. But in
order not to arouse unnecessary comment and to
avoid both unsought approbation and advice better
adapted to dissuade than to encourage, Augustine
would not retire suddenly and noisily, but continue
his lectures for the twenty-odd days between the
present moment and the regular vintage holidays.
He would then be able to retire without publicity,
and later on would not be obliged to give the authorities his true reason for resigning. He would give
another, equally true indeed, but one which in former
days he would not have considered valid save as a
means of obtaining a short period of repose. The
strain of teaching had impaired Augustine's never
very robust health, and the climate of Lombardy, so
different from that of his native country, had also
had its effect upon him. For some time he had been
suffering from shortness of breath and a sense of
oppression on his chest which made it difficult for
him to lecture at length. This condition was probably due to a slight attack of asthma aggravated by
a touch of bronchitis. He could resign therefore

on the ground of ill-health, and to Ambrose alone, at a later date, would he confide his true motive.

Moreover, he must get rid of his new mistress and release himself from his promise to his affianced bride. I do not believe that Augustine himself dismissed the concubine—the memory of past pleasures was still too fresh. A trusted and experienced friend, Alypius, in all probability, must have undertaken to rid him of the woman who, for a few brief months, had responded to Augustine's advances. The case of the young fiancée was more delicate and difficult to handle, and surely it was Monica who arranged matters amicably, Monica whose maternal and Christian sentiments would render her eloquent in explaining that Augustine's motives were not dishonourable.

News of all these happenings was imparted to Augustine's most intimate friends and disciples, and it was proposed that, all together, they should leave the city for some quiet spot and, for a time at least, lead the philosophic and cenobitic life. He could not receive baptism immediately; he stood in need of a period of recollection, of preparation, and he was eager to escape from the city's noise, to avoid indifferent or meddlesome acquaintances, and leave behind him everything reminiscent of the temptations and of the life he had so recently repudiated.

Of all the members of Augustine's circle his colleague Verecondus was the most aggrieved. Not that he regretted that his friend had become a Christian in practice as well as theory.   His own wife was already converted, but she, by the fact that she was his wife, would prevent him from joining the community Augustine and his other friends were founding.   But although he might not share the cenobitic life Verecondus, generous and attached as he was, offered the future cenobites a country house he owned at Cassiciacum—now called Cassiago—one of the most pleasing spots in the Brianza region.   Augustine was deeply and lastingly grateful to him for this offer, and never ceased to pray that he might enter into eternal bliss, for soon afterwards, in 388, poor Verecondus fell seriously ill and died.   But he was granted time before the end to become a Christian.

Another of his dearest friends who did not follow Augustine to his rural retreat was Nebridius. He had preceded Augustine on the road to truth, for before him he became aware of the absurdities of astrology and of the fundamental errors of Manichæism, and now, enlightened by the Neo-Platonists, he was become a Christian in his own way.   One error of Manichæism still clung to him, however—the theory that Mani had taken from the Gnostics.   He did not believe in Christ's humanity, and held with Marcion and other heretics that in Jesus the human body was but a deceptive appearance.   In a word, he denied the Incarnation.   Augustine argued long with Nebridius by letter, and not without effect, for later on he also was converted to the orthodox doctrine and became a Christian with all his family.

All of the others were eager and ready to leave Milan with Augustine—Monica, his relatives who lived with him, and his most faithful disciples. The vintage holidays arrived at last, and on a lovely morning at the end of October Augustine and his companions set out in happy mood for their retreat at Cassiciacum.

CHAPTER XX

THE ACADEMY IN BRIANZA

I⊤ matters little where exactly Cassiciacum was; it is infinitely more important to know what was said and done there than to identify the place topographically. It was certainly in the Brianza region, not far from the Fore-Alps and within sight of the Alps themselves. The African would never again go so far north. Nature there differed vastly from that of Numidia, and Augustine was to discover the beauties of autumn and the poetry of the mists, things new to him but well suited to quiet home life and to recollection of the spirit. The man of the south is the man of the *agora* and *forum,* that is to say of the crowd, of words, of rhetoric, of externals. That winter in upper Lombardy would incline Augustine to closer personal relationships, and to that lyric intrinsicality of abstract thought which is one of the charms of his genius.

Verecondus's villa was not actually a villa, but rather what in Italian country regions is called the *casa padronale*—the master's house—which is more often used as a storehouse than as a dwelling. Larger and finer than the peasants' houses that surrounded it, it was by no means sumptuous, as we imagine those villas to have been which the wealthy Romans owned in the Sabine Hills or at Baja. It had no garden, but a meadow stretched in front of it where stood a venerable chestnut-tree, whose spreading branches with their rich, cool foliage formed a roof beneath which, on pleasant days, the Africans held their debates.

They were a party of nine—Augustine, Adeodatus his son, Navigius his brother, Rusticus and Lasti-dianus his cousins, Trigetius his fellow-citizen and disciple, Licentius son of Romanianus, the inseparable Alypius, and the excellent Monica who naturally per-formed the duties of housekeeper and cook. Perhaps there may have been a boy—a native of the place— to lend Monica a helping hand with the heavy work, for a woman alone, no matter how capable, could not possibly have done all that was necessary for such a household. There were nine or ten mouths to be fed, although no one was earning anything. The author of the most widely read life of Augustine assumes that Romanianus provided the necessary means, especially as his son Licentius had followed Augustine, that he might pursue his studies under the guidance of his father's old friend. But I do not believe that, with all his generosity, Romanianus alone could have maintained the whole party for so many months. He probably contributed generously in consideration of his son's share in the expenses, but that was all. In the course of little less than two years of teaching Augustine himself must have laid by something; Monica also was in receipt of a small income from the tiny estate at Tagaste, and in exchange for managing the peasants, Verecondus had given Augustine permission to gather the fruits of vegetable garden and orchard. For, as we learn from the dialogues *Against the Academicians,* Augustine had been appointed to represent the owner and to oversee the harvesting of crops, and we may be sure that to obtain his goodwill the peasant farmer would share liberally with him. In this connection I may remark that the astonishment expressed by certain of his traducers is incomprehensible, who, for the purpose of casting doubt upon the sincerity of Augustine's conversion, wonder that at Cassiciacum he should have read Virgil's *Georgics* and should have encouraged others to do so also. Now Augustine had undertaken the management of a farm; he had pupils to instruct, and from his childhood he had loved the almost Christian sweetness of the great poet of Andes. Why then should he not read those works which not only were of use to the student Licentius but also contained, besides the music of the verse, information of use—even to-day—to the agriculturalist?   And wherein do Virgil's *Georgics* clash with the Gospels that teem with the husbandry of the East? Augustine's pupils studied the *Æneid,* which is now universally regarded as a sacred poem, and perhaps also the *Bucolics,* which contain the famous eclogue that made Virgil the unconscious prophet of Christ.

Moreover, it would be wrong to imagine that the villa at Cassiciacum was a monastery. Its inmates were young people enjoying a pleasant country life, who were glad to find themselves isolated and together, and who saw no sin in a smile or jest even if it sometimes occurred in the midst of the most transcendent philosophical discussion. It was an assembly of fellow-countrymen and philosophers who were united in their search for the light and beauty of truth; it was something between a brotherhood and an academy, and I use the word academy in the sense of the Platonic school, for our friends were almost without exception great admirers of Socrates' wonderful pupil, and in fact spent many hours in confuting the system of the New Academy, on the ground of its scepticism.

It was a less conventional academy than the earlier one had been—merely a large family free from all pedantic pretensions and dwelling together in harmony. Alypius was probably the most staid member of the party, and although Augustine often rallied him on the shortness of his stature, he esteemed him most highly and loved him as a brother. Licentius was somewhat unstable and fanciful; he had a passion for poetry, and was writing a poem on Pyramus and Thisbe which at times absorbed him so completely

that Augustine would be obliged to call him to order
and remind him of the superiority of philosophy over
mere poetic fables. Trigetius, who was older and
had relinquished a military career that he might
satisfy a craving for learning, was not deficient in
insight. Monica, besides her excellent qualities as a
cook, showed herself an able philosopher, and gained
warm praise from her son. Most of the others
were actors of " silent parts." Augustine himself was
both the " father guardian " and " father instructor "
of this small lay monastery, but he was a guardian who
could jest on occasion, and an instructor who was
not ashamed to learn from his disciples or from his
own wise mother. To him these first days at Cassiciacum were a time of rest and convalescence, for
not until November did those dialogues begin which
were the origin of all the works composed in the
Brianza home. After recovering his health Augustine's first task must be to study the Bible, which
he had heretofore read without sequence and his
knowledge of which had been largely derived from
Manichæan criticism or from the exegetic homilies
of Ambrose. At that time he was really familiar
only with the Gospel according to St. John and the
Epistles of St. Paul, which had so strongly affected
his conversion to Christianity. He now began to
read the Psalms, and was especially delighted with the
fourth, which begins: " Answer me when I call, O

God of my righteousness; Thou hast set me at large when I was in distress." Of this psalm so many passages must have seemed prophetic to Augustine—this among others: " . . . Lift Thou up the light of Thy countenance upon us. Thou hast put gladness in my heart."

And truly at Cassiciacum Augustine was another man. No longer was he the tortured slave struggling to cast off the last of his chains, but the placid pedagogue, comforted by friendship, strengthened by knowledge, enlightened by closer proximity to God. He could jest with Alypius, playfully admonish the rhymester Licentius, relate fables, read poetry, play upon words—in short, he had learnt to smile once more. In all of this the inevitable " diabolists " (which word, according to its etymology, means *slanderer*) have discovered grounds for denying the truth of the *Confessions,* emphasizing the contrast between the distracted catechumen in the garden at Milan and the keen philosopher of the Brianza hermitage. These critics may be learned enough in some things, but they are certainly not learned in psychology. This recovery of peace and restful cheerfulness is indeed proof that Augustine spoke the truth and that the wild storm had been followed by victory, by the reconciliation of the spirit with its God, to whom it had finally attained. Are such critics unaware that also in the spiritual heaven a season

of calm invariably follows the storm? Augustine
had always yearned for happiness, and had long since
discovered that happiness is to be found only in
wisdom, in truth; and he had come to realize at
last that this wisdom which is truth is God Himself,
and consequently that the possession of God is happiness. Now after the complete transformation of
his being he had relinquished all that prevented the
fruition of God, and had thus realized the happiness he sought. Why then should he not display
his joy in a manner that was not unbecoming? Augustine was no longer the self-complacent vagrant of
his early years or the passion-driven being of recent
times; he now held certainty, and irresolution and
the martyrdom of inner conflict were things of the
past. What wonder that his spirit should expand
after a period of such fierce tension and rejoice after
such bitter suffering? Had the contrary been the
case then indeed one might have suspected him of
deception, and had the mental perturbation which
had dominated him in Milan continued to prevail at
Cassiciacum, then should I myself doubt the accuracy
of the *Confessions*. Of what avail would the defeat
of the old ego have been had Augustine suffered
a return of depression and of spasmodic desire?

It must also be remembered that Augustine, instead of in the noisy, crowded city, was now dwelling amidst beautiful rural surroundings; that instead

of being chained down to a daily round of fatiguing professional duties, he was now free to meditate or converse at will; that instead of being tried by unfriendly or tiresome people or by persons of rank whose presence occasioned restraint on his part, he was now never separated from the mother who was rejoicing in his return to God, or from his belovèd son who was giving daily proof of budding genius and purity of spirit; that, moreover, he was living under the same roof with Alypius, his oldest and most faithful friend, and with several other young men of lively and enquiring intelligence who were able to hold their own against him in argument and also to warm his heart with their youthful gaiety—in a word, that he was living with those whom he loved and who loved him.   These various sources of happiness—and let us never forget the main source, which was his reunion with God—are more than sufficient to account for the atmosphere that pervaded the dialogues of Cassiciacum and that so exercises the minds of Augustine's modern inquisitors, either owing to their psychological ingenuousness or their philosophical acrimony.   Moreover, if during the day he jested or discoursed of academic and Platonic philosophy, Augustine certainly spent long hours of the night communing with himself and conversing with his God, and the fruits of these solitary vigils were the *Soliloquies* in which we find on one of the

opening pages that long and impassioned uplifting
of the soul to God, a very litany vibrating with love,
wherein deepest faith takes unto itself the wings of
an upsoaring pæan.

But, say these short-sighted and suspicious fault-
finders, in the three dialogues composed during the
Brianza period Augustine speaks rather as the dialectician than as the mystic, as the philosopher rather
than as the religionist, and, moreover, the second
book of the *Soliloquies* is but a dissertation on Platonic
lines concerning the immortality of the soul. The
keen thinker is there, but not yet the fervent Christian. *Calculemus,* as Leibnitz says. Augustine and
his friends went to Cassiciacum at the end of
October, and must return to Milan early in March
at the latest, for the candidates for baptism at Easter
were bound to enter their names at the beginning of
Lent, and we learn from the *Confessions* that when
the Africans set out for the city the land of Lombardy was still frost-bound. Augustine therefore
dwelt four months in Verecondus's villa, and of these
four months less than one was spent in composing the
Contra Academicos, the *De Vita beata,* and the *De
Ordine.*

Towards the middle of October, when the school
vacations were drawing to a close, Augustine wrote
to the Milanese authorities instructing them to procure a new " trader in words," as neither his physical

nor, still less, his spiritual health would permit him to go on peddling phrases and trickery at so much an hour. At the same time he wrote a long letter to Ambrose, wherein he repeated the story and confession of his errors and declared his firm resolve to receive baptism. He also enquired what books he should read to prepare himself for the ardently desired sacrament. We do not know what answer he received from the school authorities, but we do know that Ambrose replied, advising the catechumen to study the prophet Isaiah. Augustine followed this advice, but it must be confessed that the virile and powerful lyrics of the Messianic herald failed to captivate him; the book seemed to him obscure, and he soon returned to the Psalms and to his favourite, St. Paul.

It was on the 10th November, a few days after their arrival at Cassiciacum, that Augustine proposed to his pupils Licentius and Trigetius one of the problems which Greek philosophy had already striven to solve—Is a knowledge of truth necessary? Can man be happy without this knowledge? And the discussion in which, towards its close, Alypius also joined, and which was ably sustained by Augustine with Monica on his side, lasted for six days. The theories of the Neo-Academy were brought up and examined from all points of view, and the conclusion reached was as follows: " All men know that two ways lead to knowledge—that of authority and that of reason. For my part I am resolved never to abandon the authority of Christ, for no other carries greater weight." As for the way of reason he had faith that in the Neo-Platonists he would find a doctrine to serve at least temporarily, that would not clash with the Christian; but it is well to observe at once that he had already identified the Word of St. John with the God of Plotinus, and that Platonism appealed to him precisely in that he saw in it a pre-announcement and confirmation of Catholic theology. At one time Augustine had been an academic, a stoic, and now that he was enfranchised, he determined to review the ground he had covered and make an inventory of the phases that had led to his emancipation, both for the purpose of definitely expelling all trace of scepticism and to assist his friends, disciples, and readers to a clearer understanding. The work entitled *Contra Academicos,* in appearance philosophical, is in substance apologetic, in the sense that it eliminates an anti-Christian prejudice, for wherever the word " wisdom " is used it means that only true Wisdom, the God of Christians.

A few days later, on the 13th November, Augustine completed his thirty-second year, and Monica made what we may call a " spread " in the form of a dinner less frugal than usual. When the meal was over, Augustine, reflecting on the analogy between the food of the body and that of the soul, raised the question whether he be truly happy who has everything he desires. A long and lively argument ensued, Monica stating her views in strong and sensible language. Given the identity of knowledge with happiness and of the Son of God with happiness, the connection between this and the preceding dialogue is obvious. The *De Vita beata* also is, in part, a sequel to a polemic against sceptics, the rest being a demonstration of the fact that he only is happy who possesses God. It is not difficult to perceive that here we are still on the plane of orthodox Christianity, even on the apologetic plane. So true is this that the dialogue ends with a timely quotation which Monica makes from the hymn by Ambrose beginning *Deus creator omnium*, and by a reference to the three Christian virtues—faith, hope, and charity.

The third treatise, *De Ordine*, had a still stranger origin, which is worth relating. During one of Augustine's night vigils when he was deep in meditation he suddenly became aware of the noise the water was making in the channel that conducted it to a neighbouring bath, and he noticed that its sound varied, that it flowed now more rapidly and again more slowly. He cast about in his mind for an explanation of this but could find none, and he was still wondering when Licentius, who slept in the same room, annoyed by the scampering of rats, knocked on the floor with a piece of wood to frighten them into silence. Augustine, finding he was awake, asked if he had ever noticed the different sounds the water made in its channel. Licentius replied that he had, and had once thought it was due to rain, but that he had found the sound varied in the same way whether it rained or not. Trigetius, who was also awake, confirmed this, and Licentius went on to expound a theory he had formed on the subject. "It is autumn," he said, "and the leaves are falling into the channel. When there are only a few and the water flows over them without hindrance its murmuring is more gentle and clear; but when the leaves accumulate at the channel's mouth the water must strive more strongly against them and consequently flows faster and more noisily."

Augustine expressed astonishment at this theory, but Licentius assured him it was not astonishing because nothing transpires in the universe save in accordance with an order which embraces all things. Hereupon, of course, it was good-bye to sleep, and the three friends forsook their couches to start an animated conversation on the subject of this universal order, its relation to God, and its congruity to the existence of evil. Many of the most difficult problems which Augustine would solve in his later works, when he had fully developed his doctrine of theology, are here set forth for the first time with a lucidity at once complete and daring. In this dialogue Augustine shows himself even more of a Christian than in the other two, and we find in it those impassioned accents which over-critical pedants miss in the Cassiciacum writings.

At a certain point in the argument Trigetius (who had only recently relinquished his military career and was as yet but vaguely conversant with theology) made a remark from which one might infer that the Father alone and not the Son should be called God. Quickly realizing his *lapsus* he expressed the desire that the amanuensis should not record the unfortunate phrase, but Licentius mischievously insisted that it should be chronicled, thereby earning a sharp reproof from his master. Trigetius indulged in a laugh because his companion, who had not committed the error, had been reprimanded instead of himself, and at this Augustine could no longer contain himself. " What are you about? " he cried. " Are you not troubled at thought of the mass of vice and the clouds of ignorance that oppress and encompass us? Is this your devotion and ascension to God and to truth at which but now I, poor fool, did rejoice? Oh, if you could but see even with eyes as blind as mine what dangers surround us, of what a sickness this laughter of yours implies the delirium! Oh, if you could but see, how quickly, how immediately,

how abundantly you would turn it into weeping!
Unhappy beings, know you not where we are? . . .
I beseech you do not add to the load of my unhappi-
ness! My own wounds are sufficient for me, and
with tears do I pray daily to God to heal them, but
again and yet again has it been made manifest to me
that I am still unworthy to be made whole quickly
according to my desire. Do not double the weight of
my load, I beg of you . . . but as you are pleased to
call me master, requite me by walking in the paths
of virtue." Having spoken thus Augustine found
further utterance choked by tears.

This, it seems to me, is hardly the language of the
firmly grounded and serene philosopher, but rather
of the still fearful and scrupulous Christian. And
on the other hand, although the dialogues have in
general the appearance of friendly discussions of
philosophical problems like those of Cicero (and they
are in fact more speculative than intrinsically religious), it must always be borne in mind that the substance beneath the Platonic form is entirely Christian, and that not only the *Soliloquies* but the other
works as well contain frequent reminiscences of and
quotations from Holy Writ, especially from the
Psalms and from Matthew, John, and Paul. They
also contain mention of the *sacra nostra* and of the
veneranda mysteria in allusion to the sacraments and
to the teachings of the Church. Christ is spoken of

by name and Ambrose is called *sacerdos noster*. No matter what carping critics may say, both the matter and the colour of the three dialogues are Christian.

Augustine was converted, and his conversion was complete, and if he still expressed himself in Neo-Platonic terms until such a time as he should have acquired greater familiarity with the Bible and with ecclesiastical literature, it does not follow that he had stopped short at Neo-Platonism. He must clear his mind of the remnants of the past; he had been in turn a Manichæan, a sceptic, and a Neo-Platonist. In the works composed at Cassiciacum he rid himself, by means of philosophy, of all the after-effects of these doctrines, and if he preserved the phraseology of Plato and Plotinus it was only because he was persuaded that it conveyed the same truths—although not all of them—that he had found in St. John and St. Paul. Just as the seed must burst its shell to become a plant, so the seed of Christian faith which had germinated in Augustine was bursting the shell of philosophy that it might start its growth and become the majestic tree of his future theology. Soon the solitary novice would have no need of borrowed language wherewith to express his Christian thought, and already in the *De Ordine* and in the *Soliloquies* there stands revealed, besides the philosopher, the true lover of God.

Among other benefits which he derived from

Christianity was the revival of his literary productiveness. At the age of thirty-two he had written only one book, the *De Pulchro et Apto*, and between the years 380 and 386 he wrote, so far as we know, not a single page. Now, however, in a very short time, he had composed four brief works in quick succession, with eight books altogether. The period of retreat in the Brianza country had not been wasted. He returned to Milan surer of himself and of his faith, strengthened against temptation and error, and ready to submit to that cleansing for which he had longed from childhood, but which, only now when he was become worthy of it, did he thoroughly understand.

CHAPTER XXI

AS THE HART TO THE FOUNTAIN

THE hermits of Cassiciacum must return to Milan early in March because, as we know, the *electi* or *competentes*, that is to say those desiring baptism, must enter their names at the beginning of Lent, and in the year 387 Ash Wednesday fell on the 10th March. As an act of devotion Alypius chose to make the long return journey barefoot, although the ground was still frozen. On their arrival in Milan it would appear that Licentius and Trigetius went to live by themselves, but the others once more took up their abode amidst the old surroundings, where the fig-tree in the garden had not yet begun to put forth its leaves.

In those days baptism was administered only during the night between Holy Saturday and Easter morning. During Lent the candidates were instructed in all that was necessary to render them worthy to receive the threefold sacrament, for at that time baptism, confirmation, and first communion followed each other in the course of the same ceremony. In March and April Augustine went daily to one of the basilicas—probably the Ambrosian—and fortified his soul, which had become somewhat dry and confused by his philosophical ruminations, at the daily feast of the liturgy. He heard again or perhaps heard for the first time those hymns sung by the congregation, which Ambrose had composed and taught in the preceding year, when Justina's Arians and Valentinian's legionaries had constrained the Catholics of Milan to rally around their bishop in the basilica and to stand guard day and night, that the church might not be given over to the heretics. In those days of suspense and tumult the venerable patrician and statesman who had become the preacher and theologian revealed himself suddenly as a poet. The custom of singing hymns was a common one in the Eastern Church, but in the West there had been no attempt to introduce it save that made by Hilary of Poitiers, and the liturgic chant was still practically unknown. The threats of those in power, the fervour of the faithful, and the certainty of victory inflamed Ambrose's imagination, who, from a serene homilist, became transformed into an impassioned and vigorous composer of lyrics, and was soon pouring out his heart in those famous hymns which are still included in the ritual of many services. "How I wept," Augustine says, "on hearing those hymns and canticles that filled Thy Church with their sweetness, and how deeply did those voices stir me! They caressed my ear, they carried truth to my heart and roused it to loving piety, while my tears flowed freely to my infinite consoling."

Now more truly a poet than when he had strung

together verses to obtain prizes at Carthage, and
exalted by his recently acquired faith to a tender
understanding of those mysteries that inspired the
hymns of Ambrose, Augustine was undergoing a far
better preparation for the new life than the disputations of the past months in Brianza had afforded him.
Who can say with what heartfelt devotion he joined
with the choir of the faithful in singing the words
of the *Deus creator omnium,* the last verse of which
Monica had cited at Cassiciacum! " When the dark
veil of night shall have overshadowed the day let our
faith ignore the gloom, and the night be made light
thereby. Permit not, O Lord, that our spirit should
sleep, but sin only; and in the pure in heart let faith
with its cooling breath temper the hot vapours of
sleep. Freed from all impure thought let the inmost
dreams of our hearts be of Thee. Let not the peaceful rest of man be troubled by the snares of a schem-
ing enemy." No prayer could have been more
congruous to Augustine's temperament, who, even
in his mature age, was often tormented by impure
dreams.

The candidates for baptism did not frequent the
basilica for the sole purpose of participating in the
religious ceremonies, however. They also received
instruction there in the fundamental truths of the
faith, and frequently these lessons were imparted by
an exorcist to remind them perhaps that before enter-

ing the pool of consecrated waters they must cast out
the demons that lurk in the innermost recesses of the
soul. Many passages of Scripture were also explained
to them, and the *Pater* and *Credo* were commented
upon at length.

In his leisure hours Augustine continued to philo-
sophize. During Lent he began his treatise entitled
De Immortalitate Animæ, wherein, following in the
footsteps of Plotinus, he again dealt with the problem
he had already touched upon in the *Soliloquies,* going
into it more deeply still. This work is hardly a real
treatise, but rather notes of syllogisms on the
question of immortality, which had been exercising
Augustine's mind for several years. He could
give to his writing only the time that remained
after he had fulfilled his duties as a " candidate," and
he probably worked with less alacrity than he had
done in the country, for he left the composition unfinished, nor is it one of those in which his speculative
genius is most vividly displayed.

But he had not lost his desire to work and he succeeded in compiling a grammar—which eventually
disappeared from his library—and some parts of a
treatise on music. His wish was to carry out a plan
he had already set forth in his *De Ordine,* to write
seven treatises on the seven liberal disciplines, and he
tells us in his *Retractationes* that while in Milan he
sketched the outlines of those on dialectics, rhetoric,

geometry, arithmetic, and philosophy. He hoped thus to compose a *speculum* of positive knowledge, making tangible matters the rungs of a ladder whereby he and others might ascend to incorporeal realities. But of this encyclopædia of Augustine's planning only the treatise on music (*De Musica*) has survived.

Meanwhile, Holy Week had arrived, and Augustine had other things than science and philosophy to think of. According to custom, on Maundy Thursday, the 22nd of April, he recited the *Credo* aloud in the presence of the assembled congregation. That was the last day on which the catechumens might bathe and sit at meat; for the days following a strict fast was prescribed. On Holy Saturday, in the evening, Augustine again went to the basilica, where Ambrose, as bishop, pronounced the last exorcisms over him, laying his hands upon him, that his soul might for all time be purged of demons. Then, with his fellow-candidates, Augustine knelt before the bishop, his face turned towards the East, and made three solemn promises of obedience to the Divine Laws. Ambrose then breathed upon his face and made the sign of the cross upon his forehead, lips, and breast. After this ceremony the " Paschal vigil " began, which consisted of readings from the Bible followed by collects from the ritual: among others the Forty-first Psalm, which was admirably adapted to the circumstances. This is the psalm beginning:

"As the hart panteth after the water brooks, so panteth my soul after Thee, O God." The verse which reads: "My tears have been my meat day and night, while they continually say unto me, Where is thy God?" seemed written especially for Augustine.

When the vigil was over, dawn being near at hand, Augustine and his companions repaired to the baptistery where the font was, and having stripped, turned towards the East and vowed three times to renounce Satan, his works, and his pomps. Then, like an athlete preparing for the supreme trial, he was anointed with the holy oil and finally immersed three times in the baptismal waters. Hereupon Ambrose put three questions to him: "Believest thou in God the Father Almighty—in Jesus Christ the Son of God —in the Holy Ghost?" and to each question Augustine answered: "I do believe."

When he had received the three assurances Ambrose baptized the Numidian in the name of the Holy Trinity. On emerging from the pool a priest once more anointed his members with oil mixed with balsam, and when the bishop had covered him with a white tunic he again placed his hands upon Augustine's head and signed his forehead with the cross. This ceremony we should call Confirmation. Then in accordance with a custom in use only in the Milanese Church, the prelate stooped to wash Augustine's feet. Ambrose at that moment was almost on

his knees before him; he who had had no leisure to
converse with the protégé of Symmachus was now
bowed down before him like a servant; the prelate
who was on terms of familiarity with emperors now
dried the feet of him who was to become his companion at the altars of the Church, in the memory
of men and in the glories of Paradise. The two saints
were face to face perhaps for the last time on earth,
and the elder humbled himself before the younger,
the more famous before the more obscure, the master
before his disciple—both perhaps with a consciousness
of the mystical parity which the veneration of Christians and the Father's love has assigned to them.

The newly baptized were then given each a candle,
and advancing in a white-clad procession, they returned to the basilica, where the *Gloria in excelsis Deo*
was sung. This was followed by the Mass of Easter
Sunday, when for the first time they were admitted
to the Eucharistic Communion, receiving both the
bread and the wine. After Communion Augustine
was given a drink composed of milk mixed with
honey, to signify that he was now become a citizen
of the promised land, which, according to Scripture,
flows with milk and honey.

The sun had now risen to shine on the feast of the
Resurrection on that 25th April, 387. In the light
of this memorable dawn Augustine had joined the
army of Christ, wherein he would serve until death,

first in the ranks and at last as a captain. His childhood's desire that had been renewed in the prime of
his enlightened manhood was satisfied at last.

The troubled and passionate soul wherein all the
demoniac powers of evil had striven in vain to obliter-
ate the sign of the cross his mother had imprinted
upon it was restored, soothed, and flooded with joy.
The warm tears that still bedewed his cheeks were
now tears of love and of happiness. As great if not
greater than his own joy was the joy of Monica. She
had seen the threefold sacrament administered to her
son who had joined her once more in the haven of
grace that had sheltered his infancy, and although
his heart no longer belonged to her alone as in those
early days, at least she no longer shared it with a
concubine, but only with Christ Himself. Adeodatus, the " carnal son of his sinning," and Alypius
received Baptism at the same time as Augustine.
Throughout the octave of Easter the new Christians
wore the white robes in which the bishop had clad
them, and visited the basilica twice daily, for Mass
and Vespers, and also for further instruction in the
mysteries wherein they had participated for the first
time.

Early in May, however, Augustine began to think
of departure. There was no reason why he should
remain in Milan, and having resigned his professorship he was at liberty to return to the land of his

birth. Born an African it was his desire to live in Africa and for the Africans. He was already planning to found a brotherhood at Tagaste that would not be half philosophical and half religious like that of Cassiciacum, but entirely Christian. In this undertaking he was encouraged by Evodius, who was an earlier convert than Augustine, was also a native of Tagaste, and had held a position of trust at the imperial court.

Moreover, the peace that had prevailed at Milan was threatened, for the Emperor Maximus was preparing to descend upon Italy, as he did presently, and drive out Valentinian II and Justina. Soon after Easter Ambrose had left for Trèves charged with the mission and in the hope of persuading Maximus not to disturb the peace. Augustine did not wait for his return, but with his mother, his son, his brother, his cousins, Evodius, and Alypius took leave for all time of the city that had witnessed his despair and his regeneration, and set out for Ostia.

CHAPTER XXII

THE PASSING OF MONICA

THE returning party waited at Ostia for a ship to take them to Carthage. Death arrived before the ship.

As if he had a premonition of this, Augustine sought to be with Monica as much as possible. She loved all three of her children, whom " she had borne anew each time they failed in their duty to God,' but Augustine it was, perhaps, who had most fully requited her love, even when he had been furthest from her and from faith, even when he had been unclean and rebellious. Leaving her only daughter in Africa, she had followed him first to Carthage and then to Milan, like the shepherd who must find his lost sheep at all costs. She was the generous mother who gave both herself and her tears; who, instead of remaining at home to await the prodigal's return like the father in the Gospel, had travelled far by land and by sea to find him, and knew no happiness until she had seen him quaff the milk and honey at the banquet of that most generous of all Fathers.

That they might rest after their long journey and quietly await the moment of departure, Augustine and his companions took up their abode in Ostia in a small house on the banks of the Tiber, which down there, so near its mouth, is more yellow and swollen

than at any other point, and flows onward, broad
and calm, in the certainty of a speedy union with the
majesty of the sea, towards which it has been striving
since its birth on the heights of Fumaiolo. The house
had some windows overlooking a garden, and in one
of these on a June evening Monica and Augustine
were leaning, lost in contemplation of the trees below,
already laden with a promise of fruit, and of the
broad expanse of Mediterranean sky, swept by a wind
from the sea. The vast silence so warm and rose-
tinted was hardly broken by the occasional plash of
an oar in the water, and the fast-maturing fruitful-
ness of the garden, glowing with the fierce red of
poppy and geranium, reminded the exiles of the
Eden-like fields of the South and the sultry, heavy
air of their native land. But above all did this calm
and scent-laden atmosphere of spring remind the two
Christians of Paradise, as yet unseen but most ardently
desired.

Surrounded by such peace mother and son com-
muned together, and of what would they speak if not
of eternity? They were now not only one in the
flesh but one in spirit as well. All the old barriers
between this parent and child had been thrown down;
with no other being would Augustine ever feel himself so entirely one as with his mother, and at no time
had he been so closely united to her as at the present
moment.

13

The world, Augustine was saying, is wonderful, and great is its beauty in all its parts, affording to man of pure joys of light, of harmony, of health, and those also, which are less pure, of the senses. But what are all these compared to the contemplation of the one Being Who created all things, to that concentrated splendour by which we are nearly blinded? In realms above our hunger shall be appeased by that wisdom which is identical with God and which on earth we seek so vainly, seeing it but as a faint glimmer; and throughout all time we shall partake of it, for it has neither a past nor a future, but only a blessed present without end. " And while we were thus conversing and yearning for that Wisdom," Augustine goes on to say, " we did indeed touch it with the furthest-reaching fibres of our hearts; and then we sighed and, leaving those fairest fruits of the spirit suspended above us, we descended again to a consciousness of the sounds that were issuing from out mouths, where words are formed and expire."

For an instant the two saints had attained to the ineffable possession of God which Neo-Platonists called *ecstasy* and our own mystics term *perfect union*, the marriage of the ephemeral with the eternal. To Monica this moment of supernatural ecstasy seems to have brought a premonition of the end. Her mission on earth was accomplished, and she was free to soar upwards and enjoy for ever that bliss of which she had but now been vouchsafed a foretaste.

"Son," said Monica, "for mine own part I have no further delight in anything in this life. What I do here any longer and to what end I am here, I know not, now that my hopes in this world are accomplished. One thing there was for which I desired to linger in this life, that I might see thee a Catholic Christian before I died. My God hath done this for me more abundantly, that I should now see thee withal, despising earthly happiness, become His servant. What do I here?"

Writing many years later, Augustine could not recall what answer he had made to Monica's painful words, but in his heart every mother's son will know what it must have been. She had not spoken lightly. This faithful servant, her work accomplished, felt the approach of the Sabbath rest. Five or six days after this conversation and ecstasy she "fell sick of a fever" and took to her bed, never to rise again. One day her suffering was such that she swooned. Her sons hastened to her bedside and Monica, who presently regained consciousness, lay gazing about her as if seeking for something which she had but now beheld and which had suddenly vanished.

"Where was I?" she asked, and enlightened by the anguish she saw depicted on her sons' faces, she added: "Here shall you bury your mother."

Augustine held his peace, choking back his tears, but Navigius cried out, hoping to encourage her, that she must not die so far from her native land, where it would be less painful to end her days. Monica checked him with a glance, and turning to Augustine said: " Thou hast heard him! Lay this body anywhere; let not the care for that any way disquiet you. This only I request, that you should remember me at the Lord's altar, wherever you be."

Having with difficulty pronounced these words she fell silent, for she was failing rapidly. Augustine recalled how carefully she had prepared her resting-place beside her Patricius at Tagaste, that she might be united under the same sod with the man to whom she had ever remained faithful, even after she had lost him. But now, rapt by her yearning towards God, she had no thought either for her last resting-place or for her funeral, nor did she ask to be embalmed, nor that a stone should mark her grave. When someone who was present expressed surprise that she should not feel afraid to rest so far from home, she answered that " nothing is far to God; nor was it to be feared lest at the end of the world He would not recognize whence He were to raise her up."

And thus, detached from all thought save that of her future home, died Monica, at the age of fifty-six, and on the ninth day of her illness.

Augustine closed her eyes, beseeching those present

DEATH OF SAINT MONICA

From the painting by Benozzo Gozzoli, in the Church of Saint Augustine, San Gimignano

not to weep, while he himself sought to master the overwhelming sorrow that welled up from the deepest recesses of his heart. Adeodatus, Monica's grandson, "burst into a loud lament," but was silenced by the others. Christians should not mourn for their dead; they are not dead but born into true life; they are not dead, they do but sleep until the day of resurrection.

"Why then should I suffer thus?" Augustine asked himself, striving to control a fresh outburst of grief. He remembered all his mother's love and kindness, the tears she had shed; he recalled all the events of her life, even those of her childhood, of which he had heard much, both from Monica herself and from the "aged maidservant"; he grieved for all she had suffered on his account in years gone by; but he was heartened by the remembrance that of recent years she had always smiled upon him, had called him her good son, and said that never had he spoken a harsh or reproachful word to her. He thought of their sweet communing at the window, and tasted again in memory the intense delight of the ecstasy they had shared not two weeks since—yet he was not comforted.

Evodius opened his psalter and began to chant the one hundredth psalm, to which those present made the responses. Meanwhile, people had been assembling, and the house was filled with the sound of prayer. But Augustine's sufferings did not abate, and while he sought to console others and was himself outwardly calm, he was still struggling to repress the grief and tears that wrung his heart.

The funeral took place, and even in church and at sight of his mother stretched beside the open tomb Augustine succeeded in controlling his emotions. While he prayed for the dead he prayed also for himself, imploring the Father to relieve his crushing sorrow. The son of her flesh would fain have given vent to his grief in tears, but this the Christian in him forbade, in his certainty of his mother's new-found bliss. In the hope of gaining relief for his mute agony he repaired to the Thermæ, and after bathing, succeeded in getting some sleep. On awakening he felt that his anguish of yesterday was somewhat softened, and he thought of the words of Ambrose's hymn which tell of the benefits of sleep. But little by little his thoughts again reverted to Monica, to her virtues and the love she had borne him, and once more a sense of the horror of his loss overwhelmed him. She was his no longer, never again would he see her, never again hold converse with her, never press his lips to her cheek. Then at last the son overcame the Christian, and a flood of tears that would not be suppressed surged from his eyes, and his pillow was wet with them. He wept until his eyes had no more tears— wept for his mother, for himself. "And now let who will judge me as he will," Augustine writes,

" and if he find sin therein that I wept for my mother and for such a mother, let him not deride me, but rather if he be of large charity, let him weep himself for my sins and ask pardon of Christ for me."

Years ago, on a winter's day, a day of the Roman winter, all bright with sunshine, I spent many hours among the remains of ancient Ostia, going in and out of the ruined houses and from time to time sitting down to rest on a marble step or a pile of stones. Here and there a few columns still stood erect against the deep blue of the sky; but more than by the *Mitreum* or the winged Victory I was attracted by the humble dwellings where one may yet see—still intact —patches of pavement and the walls of rooms within which so many who were living beings like myself, although strangers to me and far removed, have lived, laughed, known the delights of love and the depths of despair. And to-day, as I look back on that solitary and melancholy pilgrimage, I fancy—hope indeed—that I may have stood within the walls that witnessed the passing of Monica and Augustine's grief.

CHAPTER XXIII

THE SCHOLAR IN ROME

THE Church commemorates the *dies natalis,* that is to say the death, of Saint Monica on the 4th May, but she must have passed away at a later date, for the party of Africans cannot have left Milan before the beginning of May, and the journey to Ostia took several days, especially for those who could not avail themselves of the imperial postal service. And even if they reached Ostia in May, Monica was not taken ill at once, so that her death cannot have occurred until June or perhaps even later.

What can have been Augustine's reason for going to Rome and remaining a whole year there instead of proceeding at once to Carthage? It is generally assumed that ships did not cross to Africa at that season of the year, but to me this seems improbable, unless we admit that Monica died in October, for the summer months were surely the best. Some writers have suggested that the war which broke out at that very time between Maximus and Theodosius rendered the sea unsafe, and that for this reason Augustine very prudently decided not to set sail with his boy and his friends. But the war was waged mainly on land, and what few naval engagements there were took place in Eastern waters and in the Adriatic, and we have no record of a blockade of the coast of pro-

consular Africa. Nor can we attribute this protracted delay to a desire on Augustine's part to remain
near his mother's last resting-place, for he did not
tarry at Ostia, but went to Rome soon after the
burial.

I am of opinion that the true reason for this second
sojourn at Rome was a religious one. Augustine, a
neophyte and still a novice in Catholic doctrine and
practice, felt the need of further enlightenment with
regard to orthodox theology, and of acquiring a better
knowledge of the Scriptures and broader experience
in ecclesiastical discipline. He was well aware that
his future mission would be that of the apologist,
apostle, and writer. Did he perhaps realize also that
he would eventually become a presbyter and a bishop?
In what other city, then, could he, an African by
birth but an Occidental by culture, prepare himself
so thoroughly as in Rome?

Augustine had always recognized and defended the
doctrinal and disciplinary supremacy of the Roman
bishop, and finding himself so near the fountain-head,
why should he not slake his thirst before returning
to his own country which had long seethed with
heresies? The wrestler chose to abide awhile with the
supreme master, before setting out for the scene of
his future battles.

Moreover, Rome held the tombs of the Apostles
which the pilgrims from every country already held

in pious veneration. There were also the catacombs
and the traces and memories of the martyrs. Could
a recent convert to Christianity like Augustine, who
had been dragged from the slough of error by Paul's
agency, neglect to kneel before the relics of the
founders and seek to imbue himself with the heroic
and Catholic spirit which in Rome had already overshadowed the pagan? It was in Rome also that the
world's bishops, writers, and scholars assembled, and
there it would be an easy matter for Augustine to
obtain books and acquire a knowledge of Christology
and cosmology, of which the Fathers of the Eastern
Church had been the most profound students. What
painful months these must have been for Augustine,
who, while bravely facing all the difficulties of the
new life, still grieved in spirit for his dead mother and
had much cause for anxiety concerning his own
future! He viewed at close range those *degeneres
Romani* who were to bring upon the no longer
sovereign metropolis the chastisement of the year 410;
he lived in close contact with the Church, the supreme
Church, studied its traditions and customs, and discovered that not even therein are all things perfect
and pure.

At the time of his first visit to Rome in the year
383, he had been a Manichæan and the guest of Manichæans, and so saw nothing of that which attracted
pilgrims to the city, which indeed was no longer the

metropolis of the Empire but of the Church. He came in contact neither with Pope Damasus I, Jerome, nor any other Catholic.

I believe, however, that in 388 he had the opportunity of knowing the new Pope Siricius, who had succeeded Damasus on the 17th December in the year 384. Siricius was a pope after Augustine's own heart, for he was a sturdy champion of the rights of the Roman See and of the unity of the faith, and at the same time an advocate of the mystical and monastic life. He it was who issued the first epistolary decrees wherein the right of the popes to decide what the entire Church shall accept or reject was solemnly proclaimed. His was the famous letter to the Ambrosian Church on marriage and celibacy. His was a plan for monastic discipline—all things highly pleasing to Augustine. Siricius vigorously opposed all heresies; he deplored the slaughter of the Priscillianists in Spain, but condemned Bonasus who denied the perpetual virginity of Mary, and Jovinianus who denied the importance of continence, and he also strictly prohibited the administration of the Eucharist to Manichæans.

This last point is strongly corroborative of the hypothesis that the two works, *Customs of the Catholic Church* and *Customs of the Manichæans*, were composed by Augustine in Rome and at Siricius's command. The official style is so apparent in both that they are generally believed to have been written at the request of the Catholics of Rome; and who other than the head of the Church himself could have entrusted such a task to the new champion of Catholicism? In these works the concordance of opinion between the two saints is apparent, the pontiff contributing documents that bear the stamp of authority, and the future bishop masterpieces in polemics and theological speculation.

One target against which both aimed their shafts was the sect of Mani. The *Liber Pontificalis* tells us indeed that it was Siricius who caused the Manichæans to be banished from Rome. Augustine had been an " auditor " among the Manichæans and had had every opportunity for studying their writings and knowing their bishops, and no one was better qualified than he to accomplish this task of confounding them which, even though it may not have been assigned to him by Siricius, was certainly undertaken in accordance with his desire of contrasting the moral teachings of the one and universal Church with those of the half-Gnostic, half-Zoroastrian sect.

Although he had but recently entered the maternal mansion of orthodoxy, Augustine's ready and ardent genius had already brought him to a full comprehension of its spirit and essence, so that in his treatise on the *Customs of the Catholic Church* he was in a position to pen that famous passage on the work and aims of Catholicism which, even to-day, should be kept in mind by all pontiffs and clerics, for there is no part of it which calls for modification, nor is there anything which should be added to it.   Addressing the Church he says: " Thou shalt exercise and instruct the child with simplicity, the young strongly, gently the aged, not only according to the age of the body but also of the spirit of each.   Thou shalt make women to submit to their husbands not for purposes of carnal satisfaction but for the begetting of children, and that, through united endeavour, the fortunes of the family may be advanced.   Thou shalt place husbands before their wives, not that they may take advantage of the weaker sex, but rule with the laws of true affection.   Thou shalt bind children to their parents as in free servitude, and parents to their children by loving authority.   Thou shalt tie brother to brother with the bond of religion which is stronger even than the bond of blood.   Thou shalt teach servants to be faithful to their masters, not because their condition demands fidelity, but because in the fulfilment of duty they will find happiness.   Thou shalt teach masters to be kind to their servants, remembering the Almighty Who is Lord of all, and thou shalt unite the citizens of one place with those of another, nation with nation, and in general all men among themselves, and thus not only shape society but also form a fraternal alliance; thou shalt teach kings to cherish their subjects and admonish subjects to obey their kings. Thou shalt diligently point out to whom is due honour, to whom affection, reverence, fear, consolation, admonishment, exhortation, instruction, blame, or punishment, showing at the same time that not to all are all things due, but to all is due love and to none injustice."

Herein we find set forth, perhaps for the first time, in simple but powerful language, the principle that no part of man's activity, no phase of his life, may escape the control of the Church, which is the supreme arbiter of all acts, thoughts, and even sentiments. The Church being the direct heir of the crucified Master, and in full possession of the rights she has inherited, may relinquish to no one her birthright of spiritual directorship. Her allotted task is none other than the supernatural education of the human race.

In the other brief treatise, the first of Augustine's many writings against the Manichæans, his principal aim was to demonstrate the injustice and futility of Manichæan claims against the Old Testament, and in its composition he adopts the allegorical and figurative methods with which he had become familiar in Milan through the homilies of Ambrose.

He did not abandon philosophy, however, and while in Rome wrote the short essay entitled *De Quantitate Animæ,* the third and longest part of which contains the first outline of Augustinian mysticism, his theory of a rising scale from the vegetative life which we share with the trees to the life of contemplation which unites us to God—a theory which produced those mystical "itineraries" that were so numerous in mediæval times. Thanks to Neo-Platonism Augustine had now rid himself entirely of all taint of materialism, and had attained to a conception of pure spirituality in all its richness. The multiplicity or "quantity" of the soul of which he speaks has therefore nothing to do with material space, but must be taken as signifying "power," *dinamis*. He outstrips the Plotinian conception in describing the ever-ascending manifestations, the inner hierarchy, of this power. According to Augustine these degrees are seven in number: the first is the vegetative soul, or *vivification*, which we share with plants; the second is the sensible soul or *sensation*, which we share with the animals; the third is practical life or *art* which comprehends all of our activities from agriculture to poetry and is of man alone; the fourth is merit or *virtue*, conceded only to those who prefer the soul to the body and the things of the spirit to those of the world; the fifth is permanence in purity, *gladness* or *peace of mind*; the sixth is the *entrance* or *vision* which signifies the complete transference of self into the sphere of eternal light, the final bridling of all trace of concupiscence; the seventh and last is not a degree, but the maintaining of self on the heights attained to, that is to say, in the contemplation and pure enjoyment of God. Augustinian spirituality, which is not the least luminous side of his life-work, was destined later to be enriched and to become more profound, but we shall ever find running through it the outline he sketched in Rome.

These works, composed beside the tombs of the Apostles, already contain the indication of what Augustine's gigantic and lifelong task would be—to defend the Church, to combat heresies, and to point out the means whereby the creature may attain to bliss in the creator.

CHAPTER XXIV

THE FIRST AUGUSTINIANS

AT the close of the summer of 388 Augustine left
Rome never to return, and at Ostia, where he wept
beside his mother's grave for the last time, he embarked in a ship that was going to Carthage. The
African was returning to his native land, where he
would remain until his death. Alypius and Adeodatus were with him, and at Carthage he was the guest
of the Christian Innocentius, who had been a lawyer
of the prefecture, and who, at the time of Augustine's visit, was suffering agonies in consequence of
an excruciating operation which the surgeons had
left unfinished. On the eve of a second operation
that had been declared unavoidable, the bishop Satur-
ninus, the priest Gelosus, and several deacons were
kneeling with the sick man, fervently praying that,
by some special grace, it might be rendered unnecessary. Augustine, who was present, felt he could not
join in their prayers, although he was sincerely attached to his host; but he prayed in his heart, saying
humbly: " Lord, what prayers of Thy faithful wilt
Thou answer if not these? " And when on the morrow the surgeons arrived with their instruments to
inflict further torture, they discovered to their
amazement that the fistula had healed in the
night.

At Carthage Augustine found his former disciple Eulogius, now himself a teacher, who told him of a strange telepathic dream he had had. During Augustine's absence in Milan, he himself tells us, Eulogius had been "explaining Cicero's books of rhetoric to his pupils, and one day while preparing a lesson for the morrow, he came upon an obscure passage which he failed completely to understand. This so troubled him that he slept little that night, but in a dream that came to him I myself explained the passage, or rather not I but my image, and this without my knowledge and from such a distance across the seas, while I, for my part, was dreaming of vastly different matters and was ignorant of his thoughts."

Augustine did not stay long at Carthage. He was anxious to be back in his own town that he might fulfil a vow he had made in Milan before his baptism, to give all he possessed to the poor and found a monastery. By the end of the year he had returned to Tagaste. Thirteen years had elapsed since he had gone hence to Carthage, led by his desire for fame and fortune. He returned a changed being, to find all things around him changed also. His father's house stood empty; his mother was dead; she who had been a wife to him was in hiding he knew not where; the friends of his childhood were either dispersed or grown old. But he had brought with him, in generous compensation for all these losses, the ever-ready and exalting presence of Christ. It was amongst these ruins that he set about founding the new life. In relinquishing his chair of rhetoric he had been following the example of Victorinus, his being the first of two examples that were among the instruments of Augustine's conversion. The second, that of Anthony, he had followed only in part by renouncing all concupiscence; now at last he could complete the task by relinquishing his heritage and seeking the solitude of the monastery.

Unlike Anthony of Coma Augustine was not rich; he himself has said so more than once, and we have no reason to doubt his word. Had it been otherwise would Romanianus's help have been necessary both when he went from home to pursue his studies and later when he was starting out in life? His father had left *paucos agellulos*—a few fields—nor was Augustine the sole heir. He must share with Navigius and with the sister whose name we do not know. Navigius must have been, I will not say the *succubus,* for that would be to place the elder brother in the position of the *demon*—a foolish antiphrasis—but he certainly was Augustine's docile shadow, the man of few words who feels the presence of genius, recognizes it, and holds his peace. We catch but a glimpse of him in the *De Vita beata,* when he stands by Monica's bedside; after that we see him no more.

Whether or no Navigius relinquished his share of

his father's property we know not, but he certainly
did not join his brother in the monastery, but married,
and had one son, Patricius, and several daughters, all
of whom entered convents. Of his sister Augustine
wrote at a later date that she was the superior of a
convent, and it is probable that she had withdrawn
from the world immediately on the death of her husband. The portion she had received at the time of
her marriage would, in all likelihood, have cancelled
her right to inherit, and from her would have come
no opposition to Augustine's plan. We may safely
assume that he kept his father's house, which probably
became the home of the cenobites; and it is possible
that on selling his land Augustine had stipulated for
the annual payment of a small sum sufficient to save
them from starvation. Perhaps Alypius and Evodius
contributed towards the expenses of the brotherhood,
as well as the ever-generous Romanianus.

In the beginning the convent at Tagaste counted
but a few hermits under a single head, but it was the
nucleus from which sprang the glorious Augustinian
Order which, in the course of the centuries, has been
divided into various families; it formed one of the
most dauntless companies in the regular army of
Christ, and is to-day still alive and active. In compensation for a single Luther it has given and still
gives many saints and teachers to the Church.

The house at Tagaste was not a convent in the true

sense of the word, but it more closely resembled one than the villa at Cassiciacum had done. From the outset a certain discipline must have prevailed, although it was not until later that Augustine formulated the principal rules for his monks, without, however, forming them into an actual code. There were stated times for prayer, study, and conversation; all possessions were held in common, and probably the brothers attended the divine services in a body.

For a little over two years Augustine must have led a life of partial solitude, for the monastery was founded in 389, and in 391 he went to Hippo intending to remain but a few days, and was actually detained there for the rest of his life. At this period he stood in need of time for recollection, of the leisure that would permit him to take account of himself, to study the Catholic culture of his day, to prepare himself for the long period of strife that lay before him. Those five years of life in Italy had been decisive and providential, but they had also been years of fatigue and excitement. The two capitals, Rome and Milan, had given him, indeed, far more than he had hoped for on his arrival, but they had first plunged him into a state of spiritual confusion and had later subjected him to a mental tension so strong as to have broken and destroyed one who, unlike Augustine, had not possessed a vigorous intellect and the manifest support of the Almighty, in Whom he

had at last sought refuge. Now at last he could, if
not rest (for he would never know repose until he
was laid in his grave at Hippo), at least sound the
bottomless depths of the Scriptures, reflect at leisure
on the problems set forth and too hastily solved in his
early works, finish compositions already begun, and,
above all, devote much time to introspection and
contemplation, thus rendering himself ever more
sensitive to the light of Divine Wisdom, of Christ
Himself.

In the course of these two years, in fact, he was
able to finish the *De Musica* he had begun at Milan,
to compose a work directed against the Manichæans
(*De Genesi*), a dialogue entitled *De Magistro,* and
that *De vera Religione* which is one of his early
masterpieces. But although Tagaste was a small town
and Augustine let it be known that he wished to live
in retirement, he could not avoid certain worries or
rather duties which frequently interrupted the course
of his solitary *contemplatio.* If Romanianus or some
other old friend like Lucinianus knocked at his door,
how could he refuse them admittance? Then there
were all the others—fellow-countrymen or not,
friends or opponents, Christians or pagans who needed
him. His innate kindness had been crowned and
exalted by charity, which made it at once a duty and
a delight to serve. It was well known that Augustine
had been in contact with the great; that his eloquence,

which he no longer sold to the rich, was now at the service of the poor and persecuted; that his fame had spread since he had relinquished all dealings with the word of rhetoric for love of the Word incarnate, and many indeed availed themselves of his willing kindness.

His friend Nebridius, who had not joined the brotherhood because he could not leave his aged mother, but who secretly longed to join it, wrote to him as follows at this time: ". . . And so then, my Augustine, it is true that you have the patience to attend to the affairs of your fellow-citizens, and that they do not leave you that repose which you so ardently desire. But pray who are these good people who thus molest you? They must be those, I think, who do not know what you hold most dear, what you are ever longing for. . . . I will proclaim aloud, I will protest that all your love is for the Almighty; that to serve Him and to cleave to Him is your one desire. Would that I had you at my villa where you would have time to rest. Then might your fellow-citizens cry out in vain that I had stolen you from them; I would turn a deaf ear to their complaining. You love them too well and are yourself too warmly loved in return."

Various circumstances made it impossible for Augustine to accept Nebridius's hospitality, but he maintained a brisk correspondence with him, and we still possess some of the precious letters. But Nebridius, who had become a Christian soon after Augustine and had also converted his family, died in early manhood and without seeing his friend again. Augustine was sorely afflicted by his loss, although he realized that Nebridius had attained to that perfect bliss for which they both yearned. "He now dwells in that peace," Augustine wrote, "concerning which he did so often question me, poor ignorant creature that I am! He no longer listens at my lips but at the fountain-head, with the lips of his spirit, drinks his fill of Thy Wisdom, and enjoys eternal bliss. But I cannot believe that he so far inebriates himself as to forget me, while Thou, Who art his beverage, dost remember me."

Another death wrung Augustine's heart yet more cruelly, that of his son Adeodatus, which occurred about this time at Tagaste. He had probably reached his seventeenth year, and at fifteen had already displayed talents superior to those of many learned scholars. "His genius did almost frighten me. . . . Thou didst cut short his life in this world and his memory is to me more safe, for no longer need I fear either for his childhood, his youth, or his manhood." The last reminder of his sin was removed, but at the same time he was deprived of the pride of his paternity and of sweet intercourse with a wonderful and inspiring spirit. Augustine had lived but half the span of man's allotted time on earth, yet how many empty places he already saw around him!

Adeodatus had been the interlocutor in the dialogue *De Magistro,* written by his father shortly before the boy's death. "Thou knowest well that all the thoughts I put into his mouth were his own, and he was but seventeen." This book, one of the most characteristic which Augustine has left us, opens with a searching enquiry concerning speech which forestalls the conclusions of modern analysts by centuries. According to Augustine the words we hear teach us nothing. Conversations are generally but monologues running on parallel lines. Words spoken by others bring us only such ideas as we have already derived from things. We think we are exchanging thoughts, whereas we do but exchange signs and sounds that serve to awaken the thoughts that are ours already. We receive nothing more than we already possessed. Therefore we learn nothing from the teachers—*nusquam discere.* But Augustine does not believe either in innate ideas or in the pre-existence of the soul, which, according to Pythagorean and Platonic thought, in learning does but revive a memory. But if, before its incarnation, our spirit has learnt nothing and learns nothing from teachers, whence comes the knowledge of things it does possess? There is a transcendent teacher, Augustine informs us, who by means of inner enlightenment, imparts the same knowledge both to him who teaches and to him who listens, and this Master is none other than Christ, Wisdom Eternal and Divine. Every soul has Christ within itself and questions Him, but Christ answers only according to the questioner's good or evil intentions. It is He, whether I speak or am spoken to, Who implants the same truth in the mind of him who speaks and of him who listens. This simultaneousness of inspiration might lead to the belief that there are teachers and disciples, but in reality there is but one Master—God. " Ye have but one teacher, Christ," says the Gospel, and Augustine demonstrates the profound truth of this laconic statement. This is not Father Malebranche's vision *in* God, but vision *by means of* God: *in una schola communen magistrum in coelis habemus.*

No matter what subject Augustine may be handling he always arrives, after travelling many difficult roads, at that " intellectual light that is full of love," that illumines all things, whence all things come, to which all things aspire. Even the *De Musica*, although its opening chapters are full of technical erudition, was, in Augustine's intention, an induction to mystical ascension; and even when he seems to be speaking merely as a teacher of human discipline, his one aim is to exalt the wisdom of God and render others capable of sharing in it. Ready to argue on any subject, theocentricity is ever the dominating

note in his thought.   By nature Augustine is an artist
and a poet; the last traces of his sensuality have been
absorbed in beauty.   He is well aware that for many
beauty is the best door through which their steps
may be guided towards the Divine.   Of all the arts
his favourite is song—is music.   He is not ashamed
to interrupt his most austere meditations to listen to
and enjoy the honeyed notes of the nightingale, that
invisible voice of spring, "that so sweetly doth
lament" in the gardens and groves of Tagaste.   He
had studied music from his early boyhood, and in
Milan the hymns of Ambrose, sung in chorus by the
people, had moved him even more deeply than the
great man's sermons themselves.

Of the seven treatises on the seven liberal arts he
had intended to write, the only one remaining of
whose authorship we are sure is the *De Musica,* and
even that, it seems, is incomplete.   A love of music
is often to be met with in philosophers and men of
science; that almost mathematical art, which, nevertheless, has power to stir us to the depths, is their
last concession to the world of the senses and of
passion.   Had Augustine been acquainted with Leibnitz's definition of music—*exercitium arithmeticæ
occultum nescientis se numerare animi*—I believe he
would have lent it his approval.   But to him the
teaching of music meant using the harmonies of sensation to lead the spirit to the discovery of the In-.

visible, of that Invisible which is the reason of all things visible.

The last work Augustine wrote at Tagaste was the *De vera Religione,* and to summarize it would mean to undertake a review of his entire theology. Augustine was now in full possession of Catholic truth—no longer merely scraps of truth learnt by heart and still saturated with Neo-Platonism, but truth lived and tried by the tests of experience, truth pondered with all the powers of a mind whose sole teachers were the revelations of Scripture and inner enlightenment. He was no longer the disciple of Cicero and Plotinus but of St. John and St. Paul, and of them not only, but of God Himself, of Christ, of that "Wisdom with which every wise spirit is wise." His *De vera Religione* is not only an argument against idolaters and heretics but a synopsis of Augustine's belief, an unscholastic epitome that comes, still glowing, from the forge of his heart; it is the document that confirms his complete allegiance to Christianity and the proof of the Grace that made that allegiance possible. He was no longer a pupil and a novice, but could speak as a teacher in the Church; he had put on the armour that would serve him in her defence. The humble and groping catechumen of Milan was become the learned doctor, and was on the way to becoming the saint.

CHAPTER XXV

THE SURPRISES OF HIPPO REGIUS

No man attracts the multitude more strongly than does the anchorite. Anthony of Coma was forced to withdraw ever farther into the desert to escape the swarms of pilgrims who came in search of him; and Rousseau (to cite a false saint after a true one), hiding at L'Ermitage and at Montmorency, was disturbed by the visits of disciples and of the merely curious. Solitude seems to be a state so contrary to the nature of the universe that, while pretending to admire it, the masses destroy it. The solitude of saints, moreover, is never complete, for even when men respect it, it has other visitants—divine apparitions or the attacks of demons. Augustine's was but approximate solitude; one might say he lived in retirement rather than as an anchorite, and at the desire of the people he was soon deprived even of the scant measure of freedom he had enjoyed. The rumour had reached him that there was talk here and there of making him a bishop, for his fame was spreading rapidly throughout Africa; but this prospect, which another would have welcomed with delight, did but fill Augustine with dread, which, however, was not the result of cowardice. It was that he deemed himself unworthy to fill the highest of the Christian

orders, and doubted his capacity to carry so heavy
a burden, he who had been but so recently baptized.
Whereas in the beginning he had sought renown, he
now craved obscurity.   At Milan he had dreamed of
becoming a chief magistrate or perhaps even the
head of a province, but now his whole desire was to
serve in silence the One Master and His servants . . .
to obey rather than command.   From time to time
Augustine was obliged to absent himself from
Tagaste on business connected with many matters
with which his fellow-citizens burdened him, knowing well how patient and willing he was; but rendered cunning by his very humility, he avoided on
these journeys all those places which he knew to be
still without a bishop.

It so happened that at that time, towards the
close of the year 390 or the beginning of 391, there
came to Hippo one of those high officials called
agentes in rebus, a Christian and a man of substance,
who had been told great things concerning the conversion, learning, and godliness of Augustine.   This
man, who was probably well advanced in years and
weary of the affairs of state, confided to certain
Christians of his acquaintance that he was convinced
he would have the courage to give up everything
and retire from the world to lead a more perfect
life and one more befitting a Christian, if he could
but have speech with Augustine and hear his words.

A Christian of Hippo reported this at the convent at
Tagaste, and Augustine, who had already contemplated finding a place there and transferring his
monastery, dropped everything, and without await-
ing a second invitation, set out for Hippo, impelled
by an inclination that now coincided with duty.
" He will have none other, and if I go not, he may
not be saved." Soon after his arrival he was able to
confer with the official, and sought to persuade him
to fulfil his promise; but he soon discovered that the
rich old man strongly resembled the rich young man
of the Gospel—he was ardent enough in words, but
when it came to actual accomplishment, although he
affirmed his intentions, he could not bring himself to
take the final step. He had declared that Augustine
alone could lead him to a decision, and now here was
Augustine come from Tagaste on his account and he
had had speech with him, yet he still hesitated. Knowing well by experience how slow to change its habits
is the spirit of man, Augustine was not discouraged,
and hopefully prolonged his stay in Hippo. In so
doing he was taking no risk, for this seaboard town
already had a most worthy bishop. Of course Augustine went to church with his fellow-Christians on all
Sundays and holy days, and so on a certain Sunday
must have heard Bishop Valerius inform the assembly
of his desire that a priest be appointed to help him,
for he was feeling the weight of his years, and more-

over, being by birth a Greek, he was not eloquent
in Latin. In those days not only priests but bishops
also—as had been the case with Ambrose—were
appointed by the people, so that on hearing of their
bishop's desire, the Christians of Hippo laid hold
upon the monk from Tagaste and bore him bodily
before Valerius, crying: "Behold Augustine the
priest! Behold Augustine the priest!"

At first the unfortunate victim sought to escape
from his determined captors, but perceiving that this
was impossible and that his fate was really sealed,
he burst into a flood of tears. Those who were
nearest to him concluded his pride had been hurt, and
set about consoling him, assuring him that they were
all well aware of his worth and that he certainly
deserved something better than to be made merely
a humble priest, but that he must rest content with
that rank for the present, and that from priest to
bishop is but a short step. Valerius, who knew all
about Augustine, was only too delighted to ratify the
people's choice, and thus it came about that in the
year 391, at the age of thirty-seven, the former dialectician became a priest of Christ. A place for
housing his monks was assigned to him in Hippo, and
that same year Hippo Regius witnessed the founding
of the second Augustinian monastery, in the gardens
of the *Basilica Pacis* whither, besides those who, like
Alypius and Evodius, had been members from the

beginning, there now came, one after the other, Severus, Profuturus, Fortunatus, Possidius, Partenius, Servilius, Donatus, and many others who, later on, became bishops of various African sees.

As I have said, one of Valerius's reasons for desiring an assistant was his lack of eloquence in Latin. He therefore requested Augustine to take his place in preaching the word. Augustine begged for a little time to compose his mind and prepare himself, but as early as Easter week of the year 391 he began a course of sermons which was brought to a close only by his death. This substitution was contrary to rule, for at that time only bishops might preach, and several Numidian prelates censured Valerius for his infringement of the sacred rule. But Valerius knew that in the Eastern Church priests were allowed to preach, and he was more concerned for the welfare of his flock than troubled by the disapproval of his colleagues.

Augustine, however, was not satisfied to do nothing but preach. As elsewhere, the noxious weed of Manichæism was flourishing at Hippo, where one of the ministers of that sect had established himself and acquired a numerous following. The Christians, both Catholics and Donatists, knowing that Augustine was well acquainted with this evil sect and its dogmas, urged him to hold a public disputation with Fortunatus, and to this he readily agreed. Fortunatus, on

the other hand, consented only after much urging,
for he had known Augustine many years before at
Carthage, and had but scant desire to measure his
strength against one so eloquent and so well informed
on the subject of Manichæism.   In order not to lose
standing with his followers he finally consented, however, and the dispute, which took place in August
392, lasted for two whole days. People of all denomin-
ations assembled in crowds, and notaries and stenographers with their tablets were present to take down
the words of the two champions.   As was to be foreseen Fortunatus came off badly, for as the records
show, " he could neither demolish Catholic doctrine
nor prove the truth of his own."   At last, not knowing how to extricate himself, he declared he must
go and consult with certain Manichæan bishops more
learned than himself, with regard to those points he
had been unable to confute.   With this excuse and
in a state of confusion he fled from Hippo never to
return, and as a consequence many of those whom
he had perverted returned to the true Church.

In the following year, 393, a general synod assembled at Hippo. Nearly all of the African bishops
were present, and although he was still but a simple
priest Augustine was chosen to speak on the subject
of faith and the creed. He delivered an admirable
address, which was remarkable for its lucidity and
profound erudition.   It was taken down by the

stenographers and figures among Augustine's works.

There was a custom prevailing among the Christians of Africa which Augustine could not endure—that of holding banquets in the cemeteries and churches on the days sacred to martyrs and saints. In the beginning it had been the custom to bring simple offerings to the honoured dead, but this habit had degenerated into the holding of veritable feasts, in the course of which the majority of the participants, having drunk to excess, would start dancing among the sepulchres and singing ribald songs. This was a relic of paganism that had been carried over into the new religion and appealed to the never-changing instincts of the masses, be they rich or poor. Augustine immediately began preaching against this shameful abuse, and his language was often so impassioned that his hearers were moved to tears, whereupon he himself would be unable to refrain from weeping. But once when the day arrived for one of these graveyard debauches the rabble rebelled against its suppression, saying: " We have always done this! What harm is it? " and much more to the same effect. Augustine stood his ground, however, and the scandalous custom was abolished in Hippo. He wrote a long letter on the subject to Aurelius, Bishop of Carthage and Primate of Africa, and little by little this pagan rite was almost everywhere suppressed.

In 394 Augustine was deprived of the companion-
ship of Alypius, who with Romanianus was the oldest
of his friends, and who now became Bishop of Tagaste.
The same thing might easily happen to Augustine
himself; he might be summoned any day to preside
over one or other of the many African churches, and
it would appear indeed that some such proposal was
actually made, for Valerius, to guard against losing
him, sent him for a time to a place where he would
not be easily discovered.   But the aged Bishop was
convinced that sooner or later Augustine would be
stolen from him, and he knew he could no longer
do without him.   He therefore wrote to Aurelius, the
Primate of Africa, who had known Augustine ever
since his return from Rome, begging him to raise his
favourite to the rank of bishop and appoint him his
—Valerius's—coadjutor, so that there could be no
further question of his removal.   Aurelius consented,
and so, early in the year 396, Augustine was consecrated by Megalius, Primate of Numidia.   The people
of Hippo were no longer in danger of losing one who
was labouring to re-establish the prestige of Catholicism in Africa, and when Valerius died before the close
of that same year Augustine was unanimously proclaimed his successor.   Henceforth the story of his
outward acts may be said to be that of the duties
pertaining to his office.   There would be no more
adventures, no more dramatic situations.   He would

dispute in public with the enemies of Catholic orthodoxy and take part in ecclesiastical councils, but until
the very end the greater part of his time would be
spent in Hippo, preaching to his flock, meditating on
the most abstruse of theological problems, composing
the works that flowed from the inexhaustible fountain of his genius, writing innumerable letters, helping the needy, protecting the weak, and praying by
night in his cell with a devotion that grew ever
greater.

Augustine's real story becomes one at this point
with that of his intellectual activity. In the course
of the four-and-thirty years he had yet to live the
man does not disappear indeed, but is overshadowed
by the thinker, the writer, the mystic. Now he is the
wrestler struggling with the champions of heresy;
now the philosopher testing and restoring ancient
theories and reviewing new ones; now he is the eagle
teaching how man may look upon the glory of God
without being blinded thereby, and how scale the
heights of Heaven on the pinions of contemplation.
He was always the teacher, if you will, always the
" professor," no longer of the art of rhetoric, however, but of that divine art of thinking, of believing,
of achieving purity of spirit, and becoming one with
God.

Throughout these later years Augustine is ever a
mouth that speaks and a pen that writes. He has

left us more than a hundred works, some little more than pamphlets and others very lengthy, like the *City of God,* which fills a volume. These writings constitute a vast encyclopædia of Catholic thought; they were destined to enrich the entire period of the Middle Ages, and only through abuse, bad faith, or incomprehension to give rise, in the seventeenth century, to the Jansenist heresy. Their mission it was also to strengthen the piety and theology of the Church even unto our own day, and they will live on in the hearts of all lovers of God so long as a single Christian shall remain on earth.

CHAPTER XXVI

THE BELABOURER OF HERETICS

IF you talk to the modern and ignorant "man of culture," even though he be a Christian, of the ancient heresies that for centuries swarmed obstinately and rent the Church (albeit all unwittingly serving her the while), you will in all probability be cut short by some such expression as this: " All that is archæology for the pious and for professors of patrology! Matters for the seminary! Things of the past! Sweepings of erudition! " This is an entirely mistaken standpoint. Error, although more exuberant in its forms than truth, is not infinite in its fecundity; it repeats itself, reproduces itself, is raised up again in a new disguise. Under ancient and strange appellations such as Cataphrygians, Antidicomarianites or Priscillianists we sometimes discover, to our surprise, utopian ideas, gross mistakes or false doctrines with which we are well acquainted, which many not only recognize but actually defend, and which have been revived in modern times. Some of these indeed still flourish in our midst.

If we translate them into modern terms we see at once how they may still be of interest to those who hold the ancient heresiologies in contempt, and that a knowledge of them might be useful even to the best-informed of our contemporaries,

If I begin by telling you that Augustine spent half
his life quarrelling with the Manichæans, Donatists,
and Pelagians, you will immediately scent a menace
of boredom, and feel strongly inclined to skip the
pages that follow; but when I add that, as a matter of
fact, it was against Theosophists, Protestants, and Ro-
manticists that he strove, you will prick up your
ears at once and feel that you are on familiar ground.
If, with the necessary reservations and within certain
limits, you will put Madame Blavatsky in the place of
Mani, Donatus in that of Luther, and Pelagius in
that of Rousseau, you will readily perceive that
Augustine's battlings and skirmishings are by no
means lifeless relics of a dead era but actually what
might be termed current events.

Naturally these identifications are not accurate in
every particular, but represent only partial analogies
and affinities—they are approximations rather than
concordancies.   Change the historical atmosphere,
the place of origin, the race, and the problem, and
the aspect of the heresy will change also; the theory
of eternal recurrence is not literally true even in the
world of thought.   Yet if we get down to the ger-
minal nucleus, the points of resemblance are so
numerous that these assimilations will appear fantastic
only to those who stop short at what is empirical in
historic surroundings.

In speaking of Augustine's first heresy-snaring I

stated that Manichæism was only a mixture and confusion of religions and philosophies of different origins around the old Zoroastrian dualism. Just as Theosophy becomes Buddhist in Asia with Madame Blavatsky and Christian in Europe with Steiner, so also did Manichæism assume the aspect of Buddhism in China and of Christianity in the West. Both Manichæism and Theosophy have the cunning to deaden all sense of remorse in their followers by removing direct responsibility for evil-doing—the former casting the responsibility upon the invisible god of dark-ness, the latter attributing it to *karma*—to the effects of a prior existence. But Manichæism resembles Theosophy precisely in the syncretistic manner of its composition. Epiphanius of Salamina defined it as " the polycephalous heresy," and the same term might be applied to that Asiatic mixture compounded by Madame Blavatsky and her followers. As for Manichæan dualism, we find it in other modern heretics, in Renan for example, who saw religion as a progressive victory of the principle of light and of the ideal over the principle of darkness, or matter and animalism. In another shape we find traces of the *Avesta* even in Nietzsche, who, not without purpose, gave the noisy mouthpiece of his orgiastic eructations the name of *Zarathustra*.

With Augustine the confuting of Manichæism was a matter of conscience besides being an absolute

necessity of his intellect and a duty of his office. Not
only had he himself been entangled for nine years in
the snares of Mani, but he had caused Romanianus,
Alypius, Honoratus, and many others to become
ensnared as well.   His knowledge of Manichæan
writings and customs, his disastrous propaganda, and
his own deliverance imposed upon him the obligation
of healing this intellectual plague.   He set about his
task immediately after receiving baptism in 388,
when he began his book entitled *Customs of the Manichæans,* which work was followed by a dozen more,
some long and some short.   The last, composed in
405, is an answer to a certain Secundinus of Rome,
who had written urging Augustine to renew his allegiance to the sect.   In 394 he confuted Adimantus
or Addas, the most famous disciple of Mani, and in
397, a book by Mani himself, entitled the *Epistle of
the Foundation.*   In the year 400 he once more had
to do with that Faustus of Mileve who, through his
own ignorance, had begun Augustine's enlightenment.
This man, condemned to exile, had sought to avenge
himself by composing a voluminous work containing
all the criticisms of the Old Testament put forward
by the Manichæans.   Augustine took this work seriously, and dissected it in a confutation that filled
thirty-three volumes, following step by step the text
of his former companion's book.   As we have already
seen, in 392 he had forced the Manichæan Fortunatus

to hasty flight after a disputation that had lasted two
whole days. In 398 he achieved a still greater victory. A certain Felix, who was one of the Manichæan
" elect," after disputing all one day with Augustine,
declared himself convinced by his arguments and became a Catholic. These Augustinian battles were not
mere noisy explosions of harmless powder—they
actually wrought havoc among the enemy. Manichæism was not completely routed by them, but it
was permanently weakened and impaired. Augustine
had found it in a flourishing condition, and he left it
more dead than alive. This controversial warfare
that was carried on without quarter for seventeen
years was also beneficial to the development of Augustinian thought, for it provided opportunities for for-
mulating and strengthening his doctrines concerning
the divine spirituality, the origin of evil, and the
principles of Biblical exegesis.

After the year 392, however, another heresy
brought upon itself the blows of the lusty " be-
labourer " of Hippo. This was Donatism. Rather
than a heresy it was a dangerous and turbulent schism
that had been rending African Christianity since 312.
Its origins are obscure and complex, and of importance only to a certain extent, for they belong to
the history of jealousy, malice, and politics rather
than to that of ideas. Donatism was not a doctrine
pure and simple, but the secession of a body of Chris-

tian Africans from the orthodox communion, with
the pretext that this communion had shown itself
unstable and treacherous during the persecutions of
Diocletian, too obsequious to imperial power and,
in a word, was become so debased that the sacraments
lost all value and efficacy when administered by
Catholics. According to the Donatists the Church
they themselves had founded was faultless and composed of saints, whereas the Catholic Church, un-
faithful to the heroic principles of its early days and
corrupt in its members, instead of being the New
Jerusalem, was become a very Babylon of reprobates.

I have put Donatism and Lutheranism side by side,
and with some reason, as it is not difficult to see.
From the beginning Luther's rebellion had urged motives and pretexts of a theological order, but the
chief weapon of Protestant propaganda was and still
continues to be, in part at least, the accusation of
treachery and corruption hurled against the Church
of Rome. In the opinion of both Donatists and
Lutherans, owing to the sins and weaknesses of its
heads, the Catholic Church was unworthy to represent the true and original community of Christ;
therefore they must separate themselves from this
centre of infection and set up a new religious society
in its place. Nor does the resemblance between the
two schisms end here. In Donatism, concealed beneath doctrinal justifications, there may easily be per-

ceived those nationalistic and proletarian substrata that contributed towards its success—the same movements that are to be found in the Protestant Reformation.   Donatism was the obscure rebellion of Africa against the temporal and, at a later period, the spiritual domination of Rome, just as Protestantism appealed to the budding spirit of German nationalism to oppose a foreign hegemony which again was that of Rome.

Towards the close of Constantine's reign there were formed among the Donatists bands of fanatics, peasants, and labourers who scoured the countryside, stealing and dealing out blows to the cry of " *Deo laudes*," attacking and plundering the homes of the wealthy, and taking the part of the poor in all things. They called themselves the *cumcelliones*, which some say means " those who circulate around the huts " (*circum cellas*), while according to others they were originally known as *circelliones*, which signified " the continent or chaste ones " (from *circellus* in the sense of *fibula*).   Do not these bands of roughs who, in the name of religion, abandoned themselves to brigandage and vague socialistic aspirations, remind one of the famous Peasants' War which, as a consequence of the Lutheran movement, racked Germany in the years 1524 and 1525?   Nor can it be said that a radical difference is established between Donatism and Lutheranism by the fact that the former dis-

approved of all contact or compromise with the
political power, whereas from the beginning the latter
made skilful use of the interests and ambitions of
princes, to obtain their support.   The Donatists
themselves, who loudly proclaimed the uncompromising purity of their motives (but whose consciences
were not clean even in times of persecution, as the
events at Cirta plainly showed), actually attempted
on more than one occasion to obtain the protection
of the imperial Government, and their determined
hostility was partly the result of their not having obtained it.   A comparison between the two anti-
Roman rebellions is therefore far from arbitrary.

Already in 392, while still a humble priest, Augustine had been aroused to a sense of the menace the
Donatist schism represented, and he had composed
in verse which, if not beautiful, may yet boast absolute novelty of form, a *Psalmus abecedarius contra
partem Donati,* in twenty stanzas of twelve lines each,
of which the refrain has remained famous:

" *Omnes qui gaudetis in pace,
modo verum judicate.*"

He discovered some time later, however, that a
weapon far more powerful than poetry was necessary in this matter, which became Augustine's Thirty
Years' War, for it began in 392 with a letter to Maxi-
minus of Sinitum and was brought to an end only

in 420, with the confutation of Gaudentius. More than a dozen works of his against the Donatists have survived, and Augustine's victory was crowned at the great anti-Donatist conference held at Carthage in early June of the year 411, presided over by the tribune Marcellinus. Augustine was the central figure at this conference, which ended with the final defeat of the Donatists, and was followed by the legal suppression of the schism on June 25, 411.

We may well believe that Augustine became a thorn in the flesh of these schismatics, whose bishop proclaimed him a " seducer and deceiver of souls, a ravening wolf that must be slain to save the flock," declaring also that " he who should slay this wolf would, beyond doubt, obtain remittance of all his sins." The famous *circumcelliones* were not deaf to these pronouncements, and Augustine's life must indeed have been miraculously protected, for a band of these roughs lay in wait for him whenever he moved abroad. " On one occasion," as Possidius relates, " Divine Providence so arranged that his guide mistook the way, and he and his companions reached their destination by another route, thus, through an error, as was later ascertained, avoiding the trap which had been set for them."

In his books and pamphlets Augustine never wearied of demonstrating the holiness of the universal Church, which the evil deeds of some of its members

can neither destroy nor cause us to doubt; he pointed
out the extreme weakness of the accusations hurled
against Catholic bishops by the early Donatists, declaring that the efficacy of the sacraments does not
depend upon the degree of purity of the men who
administer them, and that the Donatist Church,
which tolerated and actually favoured so many sins
in its members, could not pretend to be the Church
of Saints and of perfection. But even after their
condemnation in 411 the perfidy and violence of the
Donatists was such that Augustine regretfully invoked and championed the severe measures which the
imperial Government adopted against them, justifying his action by the *compelle intrare* of the Gospel.
Recalling the sentiments of Ambrose and of Pope
Siricius on this point he did not indeed declare that
they must be converted by force and through fear,
but that it was right to punish those who, in the
name of religion, disturbed the peace and order of
the country and the Church. But his reservations
notwithstanding, Augustine's arguments were destined to be recalled and exploited in mediæval days,
in justification of the Inquisition.

In the year 412, after his victory over the Donatists,
Augustine turned his spiritual arms against a third
heresy, that of the Pelagians. Pelagius was a monk,
and like Abelard and Renan, a native of Brittany,
who lived in Rome at the beginning of the fifth cen-

tury, and with the valiant aid of his disciple Cœlestius spread his doctrine throughout Sicily and Africa, whither he betook himself in 410. Two councils, held at Carthage and Mileve in 416, denounced the new heretics, and in 417 Pope Innocent I condemned Pelagius himself.

I have mentioned Rousseau in connection with Pelagianism, for Pelagius's doctrine is, in fact, but a Christian disguise for the ancient historical theory and, at the same time, an anticipation of the fundamental thesis maintained by the author of the *Discours sur l'inégalité*. The Pelagian held that of his own will man can accomplish all things, and that he may attain to virtue and achieve salvation without the help of Divine Grace. Christ did not come to redeem us from original sin and therefore from death itself, but merely to set us an example and to raise us to a higher life. Original sin does not exist. Adam's sin affected only himself, and had no influence on his descendants. Man is born pure and virtuous as was Adam before he sinned. Baptism is not indispensable nor is prayer. We can be saved through obedience to the moral law as well as by the Gospel.

It is clear that this was to void Christianity of all mysticism, was the negation of some of its fundamental principles—redemption, original sin, the efficacy of baptism and of prayer—and its reduction to a

16

sort of lay or stoical creed founded on a nominal devotion to Jesus and on the assumption of the natural
innocence of man, which creed is strongly reminiscent of the *Profession de foi du vicaire savoyard* of
Jean Jacques, that patron of the romantic rehabili-
tators of the innocence of our passions. The controversy that Augustine carried on against this radical
alteration of Christianity began, as has already been
stated, in the year 412, with his *De Peccatorum
Meritis,* and ended only with his death in 430, which
interrupted a work he was writing against Julian of
Eclanum, the great systematist of the heresy. In his
De Natura et Gratia and other works this controversy
afforded Augustine's theological genius opportunities
for elaborating and developing his famous theories of
grace and predestination based upon a radical pessimism which would seem to reduce the entire human
race to a " condemned mass " out of which God, for
inscrutable reasons of His own, saves only those whom
it pleases Him to save. These theories, misinter-
preted and distorted, were revived in the seventeenth
century under the name of Jansenism.

What troubled and offended Augustine most in
Pelagianism was the pre-romantic doctrine of the
original innocence of man. He was well aware from
painful and sinful experience how man, even in childhood, is pursued by every form of lust, and above
all by the lust of the flesh. To hear Pelagius and

Cœlestius calmly proclaim that man was virtuous by nature and that his own will was sufficient without any supernatural remedies to maintain him in a state of innocence, seemed to Augustine, as it seemed to the Church, a piece of foolishness based on complete ignorance of the human soul, and a jumble of anti-Christian errors as well; and as was but natural, impelled by his zeal in uprooting it, he arrived at the point of sustaining theories that almost touch the other extreme. Had the pessimistic dualism of Manichæism been reawakened in Augustine, as Julian of Eclanum declared? This cannot be definitely assumed, for Augustine recognized man's part in the work of salvation, although he deemed it but a small part and one ever subject to Divine Grace.

One thing is certain, however, that the heresies were not without their influence on the development of Augustinian doctrine. It was, for example, the Donatist Ticonius who gave him the idea of placing the two cities—of Satan and of God—in opposition, and who gave him also the rules of Biblical exegetics. St. Paul says that heresies are necessary; not only do they force the orthodox to a clear defining of true doctrines, and gradually to formulate dogmas, but they are also a sign of the vitality of the faith. The worst enemy of religion is not heresy but indifference, scepticism. A church without heretics is a church fossilized, one that has become merely a devotional and juridical institution.　　But heresies are of use only when they are fought against, overcome, and conquered, and therefore Augustine, who was the most heroic fighter of his day, owes to the heretics some of his most profound thoughts and a part of his glory.

CHAPTER XXVII

THE EPISTLE TO GOD

IT is with Augustine as with celebrated cathedrals
that are more often admired from the outside and
from a distance than visited for the sake of their
broad aisles and gloomy crypts; but if any one work
of his is read we may be sure it is the *Confessions*.
The *Confessions* have as much right as have the
Odyssey or *Paradise Lost* to a place in the inventory
of universal literature. Together with the *Imitation
of Christ* and the *Divine Comedy* this is the most
widespread of Christian works; throughout the Western world the *Confessions* have been repeatedly
translated, annotated, and reprinted, and this work
is one of those even agnostics and unbelievers feel it
necessary to read. In mediæval days the *City of God*
may have been even more popular, because those
dwellers in the shadow loved bright monuments of
stone as of thought; but to-day the *Confessions* hold
the field for popularity. We are become the investi-
gators, sometimes, indeed, captious and irreverent, of
the lives of others; psychoanalysis interests us more
than the philosophy of history—we have grown less
metaphysical and more psychological.

Augustine was richer than we are; for he was the
last of the great metaphysicians of antiquity and the
first modern psychologist. Whereas in his other works

he appears only as a battering-ram for the demolition of the bastions of heterodoxy, or as a cyclopean architect, in the *Confessions* we have speculation and introspection, theology and autobiography, God and the ego. In our day most readers search the work only for this last, and especially after the ninth chapter their teeth are on edge and they pull a wry face. They have been looking for a dismembered soul, and instead find themselves transported on to the heights of prayer.

A misunderstanding separates Augustine from the moderns. The word *Confessions,* used by so many, has a different meaning for him than for us. Augustine had no intention of writing his memoirs, his autobiography, as so many, inspired by his example, have since done. *Confessio* to Augustine signified indeed the recognition of his sins, but above all the extolling of the mercy, grace, and wisdom of God. He took *confiteri* in the Biblical sense: " I confess Thy glory and bear witness to Thy power. I am therefore essentially something in the nature of an offering." *Accipe sacrificium confessionum mearum,* he writes at the beginning of the fifth book. More than an autobiography, the *Confessions* are an ascent towards God, a continual declaration of love for God. The story of his past life is told by means only of the most indispensable facts, and solely because it constitutes a proof of the power of Divine Grace, and bears apologetic witness to what God did in illumining one who was blind, in cleansing one who was unclean. There are, it is true, two forms of confession—one of praise and one of accusal—but this second form, which is necessarily personal, is part of the first, in that it is a proof, a corollary, of the other, is implicit in its function.

To whom then should he make confession in the sense in which we understand it? Certainly not to God Who knows all things; this would be but superfluous repetition. To his fellow-men, then? But as a catechumen he had long since confessed to Ambrose and Simplicianus, to whom he had revealed all the sin and error of his life before baptism. He certainly writes also for his fellow-men, nor is he ashamed to lay bare the inmost secrets of his being, even to the scars left by the leprosy which had once defiled him; and this not for the purpose of satisfying his readers' curiosity or from motives of empty vanity, but in the hope of serving as an example to other wayfarers, and of obtaining the prayers of his brethren.

Augustine himself has stated his true purpose in his *Retractationes*. " The thirteen books of my *Confessions* praise a just and merciful God alike for all my blessings and for all that in any way affects me; they lift up the heart of man to Him." The purpose then of these, as of all Augustine's works, is theocentric. Had it been possible to avoid mention of self he would

gladly have done so, but as his own case constituted
a fresh document in the archives of Grace, he was
induced to relate as much of his past as he considered
indispensable. If his writings had any other purpose
than to glorify the Almighty, it was certainly the
very opposite of ostentation. Possidius, who was with
him until the day of his death, tells us that he was
moved to write the *Confessions* by the desire that
" no one (in the words of the Apostle) might esteem
him to be other than what he knew himself to be,
and also that he might reveal the nature of true humility; not to spread deceit, but to praise not himself but
God for the blessings he had received by his liberation,
and to obtain further blessings through the prayers
of his brethren." He did not write them to clear
himself of the accusations brought against him by the
Donatists, as Erasmus supposed; rather indeed, by
this work did he place a weapon in the hands of his
accusers!

Such an undertaking, carried out for the purpose
which was anything but autobiographical, was something entirely new at that time, especially as regards
the manner of its accomplishment. The ancients
shrank from writing of personal events save for purposes of self-glorification or justification. It was the
solemn Aristotle who declared that the perfect man
" speaks never either of himself or of others." This
precept was not always observed, but those ancients

who did write of their own doings, even when, like
Xenophon and Cæsar, they spoke in the third person,
did so for purposes of self-exaltation or, as was the
case with Æmilius Scaurus and Cicero, in self-de-
fence.   Always, however, they dealt with outward
events only, and never with spiritual vicissitudes,
whereas the *Confessions* of Augustine, like the work
planned by Leopardi, may be justly termed the *History of a Soul*.   Augustine's sole predecessor in this
respect was Marcus Aurelius, but his *Communings
with Himself* are as far removed as possible from the
Confessions.   They do not form a dramatic recital,
but are merely a list of recognized obligations followed by fragments of general reflections and of
advice, and by quotations from books he has read.
In Marcus Aurelius we find all the cold complacency
of the stoic in the making; in Augustine all the fire
of the soul redeemed, which accuses itself in order to
praise its God the more.   Not even that cold and
brief autobiographical poem by St. Gregory of
Nazianzus can stand side by side with the African's
soul-shaking polyphony.

In this work it is the inner man who has sent forth
upon the lava stream of a very pæan of glorification
all his apprehensions, his flights towards the central
fire of the universe, his longing to penetrate to the
deepest depths of being.   Glimpses of sensuality,
flashes of ecstasy, inner turmoil, intellectual rebellion,

all the vigorous germinations of a luminous and fiery spirit, render this dazzling complex clear and miraculous. If according to Keats's profound definition the earth be the " vale of the soul's creation," this book is the earth, is a world. Herein we are shown a soul being gradually healed by the mercy of the Supreme Physician; a soul that is finally raised out of the slough of sensuality to intoxicate itself at that great feast with the wine of the eternal light. Augustine becomes the subject of his own denunciations and while his ardour in stripping himself bare leads to the revelation of many thorns embedded in his flesh, his ultimate purpose is but to prove that every thorn may become an oar or a wing. We behold him, who in his youth had been but a vendor of empty words, become before our very eyes " the table of bronze whereon the Lord doth write."

Like the *Divine Comedy* and the *Pilgrim's Progress* this is the story of one who, sustained by Grace, soars upward out of the forest of error and attains the spheres of salvation and contemplation. It is not founded on the seed of Adam divided into three kingdoms or upon an allegorical and mystically conceived chart, but upon a world of ideas and passions that is entirely human. The scheme of thought, however is identical; a metamorphosis from the depths to the heights, a " comedy " with but two actors—God and the ego—which has a happy ending.

The work cannot be classified. It is not biography, of which it lacks many attributes. By turn it is an outpouring of emotions, an oration, the teacher who explains, the philosopher who cogitates in our presence, the theologian who instructs, the poet who loses all sense of suffering in the chaste beauty of what he himself has evoked, the mystic striving to express the inexpressible.

If to any class, the work belongs to the epistolary. In writing Augustine must always feel the presence of some being, must know to whom he was speaking. He never discoursed to empty space or spoke in general terms to unseen listeners scattered amongst the world's anonymous. In his polemical tractates he addressed his adversary; in his dialogues his interlocutor; in his letters his friends; in his sermons the faithful. Each one of his works bears on its title-page a name and an address. And what are the *Confessions* but a vast epistle addressed to God, a magnificent letter from the slave to the Master, from the redeemed to the Redeemer, from one who is ignorant to the All-Wise, from one who has received to the Benefactor? In Him he confides, of Him he asks, Him does he remind of past mercies granted, to Him commends his welfare; and as if he were writing to a powerful friend so does he proffer his request, and Him does he love above all others. A careful examination of the work will show that persons are mentioned in it only when they serve to throw light upon what concerns the writer; the *Confessions* loom in vague and empty space wherein we perceive only Augustine and God—Augustine below, on earth, addressing God; God in His Heaven apparently now the mute listener, but One Who has already spoken through the light of Grace. The book is a letter that was answered before it was written; a hymn of thanksgiving laid by the beggar at the feet of the Rich Man who has fed him.

In the *Confessions* Augustine removes, one might say, tears off with violence, the several garments in which his daily life is clad, so that nothing may remain between himself and God, and although here and there, and especially at the end, the exegete, the theologian, or the philosopher may appear, this book remains the true mirror of his inner man, his examination of conscience in the presence of the Absolute. To Augustine the word Christian did not signify something added to *man,* but was the explanation and necessary complement of man—one and the same thing. This must disprove the opinion of those who would see in the *Confessions* an Augustine who creates bodily, almost out of pure fancy, a " religious experience " which he superimposes upon his true ego. For Augustine man without God cannot be truly alive, cannot be himself; therefore it is man's duty to dwell, in so far as is possible, in His presence, in

His company, let us even say, in closest intimacy with Him, would he indeed exist. Once at least, shutting out the controversialist and the bishop, Augustine would fain be alone with God, would speak with Him alone, and feel himself living in God.

To God Who knows all things all may be told, even what is hidden from the eyes of men, and the shameful secrets of our spiritual poverty, which, even after the greatest of gifts, is still immense.

Many who resist conversion imagine that what they term the " new man " comes into immediate being in the convert, and failing to find him as radically altered as their ignorance has led them to expect, they promptly deny the honesty and substantial nature of the conversion. The example of Augustine, that world-famed convert, should suffice to enlighten them. The most complete conversion does not, cannot, suppress man's inborn nature—the old man. It reforms this nature, prunes it, exalts it, but does not destroy it. Those forces that inclined towards evil it turns to good, but they remain the same forces in so much as they are powers of the spirit and the mind; those intellectual faculties which were once satisfied to remain in error are now used in the service of truth, but they are still the same faculties, not weakened but rather become more vigorous, yet still the same. The soul alters its direction but not its nature. He whose tendencies were towards wrath, intolerance, pure theory, impassioned controversy, remains what he was before, with the important difference that he now uses those tendencies for the greater glory of God and not in the service of the devil. Augustine, who had been a master of rhetoric and a lover of philosophy, remained a philosopher even after conversion, and in style a rhetorician, but his learned eloquence and his ability as a philosopher were now used in defence of Christ instead of in serving Manichæanism or in the pursuit of fame and riches.

Nor indeed are actual vices immediately and completely expelled. They are checked and curbed, reduced and weakened, but in one form or another, even in the presence of sanctity, they will seek to reassert themselves. The depth of the change may be gauged by the fact that whereas of old vices were tolerated now they are abhorred; whereas formerly they were not regarded as vices they are now seen in all their foulness; whereas at times they were once openly gloried in they are now felt to be a load of shame.

Here again Augustine bears conclusive witness. He wrote his *Confessions* in or about the year 397 or 398—nearly twelve years after his conversion. Yet in the analysis of his soul in its present state, which he makes in the tenth book, after he has related the events of his past, we find the transformation in course of progress indeed, but still incomplete. The sinner is not yet become the saint, but is still troubled by certain sinful tendencies of his old nature which, although they no longer triumph, yet are not destroyed. He himself recognizes this: " Thou didst *begin* the change in me, and dost know in what *part* I am altered," he says.

To him at four-and-forty, priest and bishop as he was, life still offered temptations *sine ullo interstitio*. The sensual tendencies which had assailed him early in life and so long prevented his return were not dead within him; he had renounced them, but they still assailed him. The images of those delights which had long been habitual " are but weak in my waking hours, but in my sleep they bring me not only enjoyment but even to the point of acquiescing and to the illusion of the act itself."

It is not possible to give up food as one may give up woman; one may eat little, but nourishment one must have; and it quickly became apparent to Augustine that sensuality always accompanies the act of satisfying this need, although less in drinking than in eating. The concupiscence of the ear made him too fond of music, even of church music, and at times he was more deeply moved by the sweetness of the singing than by the meaning of the hymn itself. His eyes also were overfond of the beauties of creation, of shapes, of the specious in art; *libido sentiendi* driven out at one point, was again attacking under a more decent but still sinful disguise. And the pleasure of looking, of observing, of seeking, justified before one's conscience by a desire for knowledge, but which all too often is but delight and the satisfying of idle curiosity! Even in his old age, as he had done in his childhood, Augustine delighted in watching the dog in pursuit of the hare, the lizard snapping at a fly, the spider spinning its web for the undoing of its victims.

There were times also when he realized that he was acting for the satisfaction of man's twofold desire to be both loved and feared; he was tempted through self-complacency, and despite all his efforts not to do so, he accepted praise more readily than he should have done. The three fundamental lusts—voluptuousness, curiosity and pride—those lusts which Dante would one day discover in the three beasts of the forest, had been blunted and condemned in Augustine, but they had not been severed at the roots and were perhaps ineradicable. The new man had been born in him but had not slain the old man. The old Adam was in part enchained and in part exalted, but he still existed and at times rebelled. In the early books of his *Confessions* Augustine seems to be saying: "Who can console me for my past happiness?" Now on the verge of old age, he asks: "What punishment can suffice to render me worthy of the fullness of future bliss? "

" Too late I loved Thee, Thou Beauty of ancient days, yet ever anew! Too late I loved Thee! " Such is the despairing cry of the man new born. After so many years of works and prayers, of purification and ecstasy, he knows he is still imperfect and wretched. " We make manifest to Thee our love by confessing our wretchedness and praising Thy mercies, that, having *begun our liberation, Thou mayest free us entirely*; that we may cease to be wretched and know bliss in Thee."

In Augustine we find the mark of true sanctity, which is not believing oneself a saint.

17

CHAPTER XXVIII

THE TWO CITIES

WHEN Alaric was born in the year 370 at the mouth of the Danube, the offspring of a great Visigoth family, no one could have foreseen that this child would unconsciously inspire one of the most ponderous and heroic works that was ever written—an epic both historical and mystical, in whose composition it may truly be said that heaven and earth, man and God, participated.

The Goths were barbarians, but as early as 275 they had been incorporated in the Empire, and since the beginning of the fourth century many of them had been Christians. Alaric himself was a Christian, but the Gospels, which he was able to read in Ulphilas' translation, had not destroyed in him the warlike *libido* and barbarian ferocity. From early youth a soldier, he served Theodosius against Eugenius with bands of his own people, but having displayed dissatisfaction with the remuneration received, he was dismissed from the service. He had already acquired the nickname of Balta, the Daring, and he demonstrated his audacity by laying waste the Peloponnesus and conquering Athens after the death of Theodosius. In 397 he settled in Epirus, but could not rest content with so poor a country, and in 401 he invaded Italy, laying siege to Milan. Stilicho, Arcadius' great barbarian general, of whom Claudianus sang, defeated him at Pollentia and again at Verona, but he returned to Italy in 408, besieged Rome, and levied a heavy toll on the unhappy city. In 409 he was back in Rome once more and raised her Prefect, Priscus Attalus, to the rank of Emperor, only to depose him again presently when he had hopes of coming to terms with Honorius. Disappointed in this, he returned a third time to encamp beneath the Aurelian walls, and on August 4th, 410, succeeded in forcing the Salarian Gate, whereupon for three days his soldiers, who were the scum of all races, put the metropolis of the Empire to the sack. On the 7th or 8th August, followed by a long train of carts laden with the spoils, he set forth from Rome and moved southward, intending to take ship and proceed to the conquest of Africa. This Visigoth, who was not even a king, stood forth for a time as master of the Western Empire; but punishment followed close on his evil deeds. Having reached Calabria he was about to set sail for Sicily, when he was overtaken by sudden death. In accordance with their custom the Goths turned the river Busento out of its course that they might bury in its bed the body of this Alaric the Daring who had thrice violated the Eternal City.

The sack of Rome stirred and terrified the entire Empire; even St. Jerome in his hermitage at Bethlehem was distressed by the news of it. Whole quarters had been destroyed by fire; so numerous were the corpses that their burial was a heavy task; the superb palaces of the patricians had been invaded, plundered, and set on fire by the drunken barbarians; all virgins, both Christian and pagan, had been violated, save those who sought safety in death, and several churches —albeit in defiance of Alaric's orders—had been put to the sack. But most terrible of all was the humiliation the city had suffered. Not for eight hundred years, not since the taking of Rome by the Gauls in 387 B.C., had the capital of the Empire been invaded and outraged by barbaric hordes. Several times indeed in the course of the centuries the city had been threatened, but it had always been spared invasion. Rome had faith in her invulnerability, in her sacred character, in the protection of the gods Æneas had brought from Troy and in this new God Peter had brought from Jerusalem. Her surprise, then, was greater than her terror, and her shame greater than her surprise.

In Africa the effects of the sack were keenly felt, for many fled thither from Italy—Pelagius among others—cherishing the hope, which within a few years proved vain, that the barbarians would never be able to invade that province. In his sermon *De Urbis Excidio*, Augustine echoes the terror of the fugitives. The impotent wrath of the pagans was poured out against Christianity. So long as the

ancient gods had been honoured, they said, Rome had
not only been spared but had been everywhere triumphant; but since the emperors had taken to favouring
those miserable sectarians, followers of the Galilean
agitator who had died a thief's death on the cross,
everything had gone wrong. Theodosius's latest
edicts, which aimed at overthrowing the last stand
of paganism, had roused the anger of the ancient gods,
and Alaric had been the injured Jove's revenging
hand. Christianity had brought bad luck.

As early as the year 252 St. Cyprian had had to face
similar accusations when a certain Demetrianus
blamed the Christians for a pestilence which afflicted
the Empire for twelve years. Among other arguments Cyprian had urged that, on the contrary, God
was indignant because the Christians were being persecuted. A few years before the promulgation of
the edict of Constantine, Lactantius had promised
that if the Empire became Christian the golden age
would return. But now, when Christianity had
ceased to be persecuted and yet the golden age had
not returned, the ever-increasing power of the
Church notwithstanding, when, indeed, the besetting
evils were becoming ever more numerous, these re-
torts no longer carried weight, and the surviving
pagans triumphed.

Conscious as he was of the threatening nature of
these murmurings which the disastrous events of the

year 410 had strengthened and apparently justified, Augustine hastened to battle with them. Some of the Christians of Hippo, timorous as others have been in all times and places, would have had him refrain from any mention of the subject: *O si taceat de Roma!* they said. But Augustine refused to be silenced, and in his letters and sermons continued to proclaim that not the religion of Christ but the Romans themselves were responsible for their misfortunes. These views, however, expressed to a limited number of listeners, lacked the power to stem the anti-Christian reaction that was becoming tumultuous, and in 412 or 413, at the request of the tribune Marcellinus, Augustine embarked on the mighty task of composing his *De Civitate Dei*.

Goethe has said that the finest lyrics are those that are topical. The two-and-twenty books of the *City of God*, which, in my opinion, form the most prodigious of prose epics, were the outcome of an event, and would perhaps never have been written had it not been for Alaric's undertaking. The sack of Rome was but the incentive; starting from that episode, which was by no means unique, for thousands of cities have been sacked throughout the ages, the soaring genius of Augustine produced a synthesis of the history of man and of the Divine, wherein our human species, divided into two camps, wages war beneath the eye of the Almighty, and he created a vision which for a thousand years illumined and shaped Christianity.

This densely crowded work contains an apologetics, a theology, a philosophy of history, and a moral code; it starts with the sacking of a city, and ends with the resurrection of the bodies of the victims beneath the new heavens; it treats of the time when earth was not yet, and ends when earth no longer is; it is the history of a war and teaches peace; it deals with human events, and God is the chief actor. It is at once an epic and a drama; the struggle is not between the hero and fate as in Greek tragedy, but between man and Satan, between man and God. It is a drama and an encyclopædia; it contains all the knowledge of antiquity, the customs of barbarians and the systems of the philosophers; the darkest superstitions and the wars of empire; the hierarchy of the angels and anecdotes of the time. It is an encyclopædia, and at the same time a mighty theological treatise; all the dogmas of Christianity from original sin to the resurrection of the body are defined and demonstrated in it.

Although the work was fourteen years in the writing—for Augustine, already advanced in years, had a thousand other occupations besides—and although it is thickly strewn with *excursus,* as a whole its architecture is harmonious and reminiscent of that of the basilicas of Constantine. The first part, a sort of splendid atrium, consists of ten books, which constitute a most complete confutation of Roman tradition and of pagan mythology. The first five books contain a review of Roman history which is intended to show that the gods are incapable of assuring good fortune even in this world; in the five others paganism is reviewed in both its popular and philosophic aspect, to demonstrate how it fails to ensure happiness even in a world to come.

The second part of the work, consisting of twelve books, goes to the core of the matter, taking up the history of the two hostile cities—the terrestrial and the celestial—and is itself divided into three parts of four books each: the first (XI-XIV) tells of the cities' origin; the second (XV-XVIII) of their existence through the centuries; the third (XIX-XXII) of their final destinies, the terrestrial or Satanic in hell and the celestial or divine in highest heaven.

The central idea is the juxtaposition of the two *civitates, Civitas Dei* and *Civitas Diaboli.* "Two loves made the two cities—the earthly or love of self which leads even unto contempt for God, and the celestial, the love of God which leads even unto contempt of self. Moreover, the first doth glory in itself and the second in God. For the first doth seek the glory of man; but for the second God is supreme glory, the witness of the conscience."

The first city then is of the righteous, of the com-

munity of the elect, of those who yearned towards
Christ and of those who cleave to Him; the second
is of the wicked and of the tribe of the unrighteous.
The first is not precisely the Church, but sometimes
becomes identified with her; the second is not precisely
the pagan state, but often coincides with it.

The city of God is founded upon love; the City of
Satan on hate, because it is incapable of achieving
even perfect human justice. To the citizens of the
City of God this world is but as a poor road-house,
for true life, the life of happiness, begins only after
death; for citizens of the terrestrial city this is the
only real world, and on this world they lavish all the
affection of which they are capable, but for them a
second dying will follow death.

Augustine's mind was destined to remain to the last
radically dualistic. Like all mighty souls he knew
not the zone of greyness. His eyes saw but the
boundless sapphire of Heaven or the awesome glow
of hell. This continual strife between good and
evil may appear reminiscent of Manichæan dualism,
and the subject of the two hostile cities had indeed
been suggested to him by Ticonius, the only Donatist
Augustine held in esteem, who was eventually excom-
municated by his co-religionists. Out of these elements that were tinged with heresy, Augustine
brought forth one of the great masterpieces of
Catholic orthodoxy. The wicked will exist even

unto the end of time, therefore they are indestructible, but they are conquered and held in the bondage of eternal punishment. God is one only, and for ever victorious. The struggle is between the good angels and the bad, between the righteous and sinners, but the division is not of God's creating, although it is a consequence of the divine and dangerous gift of free will He bestowed upon His creatures. Since the time of Eve men have had free choice, and those who chose evil are the natural and perpetual enemies of those who chose righteousness. In the present life the two classes mingle and live side by side, but in the life to come they will be separated for all time by the final judgment.

This gigantic theanthropical drama, like those of the tragedy of antiquity, may be divided into five acts. In the first God creates man (Adam) in His own likeness. In the second man seeks to become God's equal and instead becomes less than man (the fall). In the third, by means of the Law, God teaches him how he may once more become man, but man shows himself incapable even of attaining to justice, and becomes bestial. In the fourth God (Christ) invites man to return to *holiness*, that is to become once more *similar* to God. In the fifth a portion of mankind withstands the temptations of Satan and yields to the temptations of Christ, and such shall live for ever in a state of bliss (the City of God) ; the others who turn a deaf ear to Christ's invitation become ever less God-like, ever less human, ever more bestial, and they shall live for ever in eternal torment (the City of Satan). Creation, Fall, Revelation, Incarnation, Resurrection.

So long as they are on earth the citizens of the two cities may be interchanged; by apostasy an inhabitant of the celestial may pass into the terrestrial, and even a slave belonging to the terrestrial may, through conversion, gain the celestial. But after death the fate of each human being is sealed, and no exchange is possible. This, in different words, is the scheme of thought laid down by Augustine for his work.

Like every literary creation that is genuinely Christian it seems revolutionary. In the place of the old *virtus* that was the ideal of the men of old, it puts *charitas*; the tradition of conquest—the national tradition of Rome—which is but brigandage on a broad scale and legalized plundering, is supplanted by the renunciation of worldly goods and the conquest of Heaven; the history of Rome that had once seemed an epic of glory appears as a recital of shameful deeds; the present life, which to the pagans was everything, to Christians is but the patient preparation for life eternal. Old distinctions are suppressed; Romans and barbarians, Greeks and Africans, the quick and the dead, all belong to one or other of the two cities. Ancient civilization was founded on the separation of castes and races; the new, the Christian, civilization recognizes only the just and the unjust, the elect and the reprobate, servants of Christ and servants of Satan. The old values are reversed; the City of God is the condemnatory epitaph of the monstrous Græco-Latin corpse, and the birth certificate of Christianity. It was not by mere chance that Augustine's work became the favourite reading of Charlemagne, the founder of the Holy Roman Empire.

But the Frankish king was not the only one who drank from this clear and mighty stream. " For the first time, in this work," Gilson writes, " thanks to the light of revelation that made manifest to it the origin and hidden purpose of the universe, human reason dared to attempt a synthesis of universal history." With his *City of God* Augustine created the philosophy of history. Bossuet derived his *Discours sur l'histoire universelle* directly from this work, drawing freely upon it. Modern philosophers may criticize this theological and teleological conception of the history of mankind, but the hypotheses which they suggest are even less convincing than the sweeping visions of Augustine, who does not explain man by man alone, and sees in the conflict between the just and the wicked the deep-seated motive-power of history. It has been said without reason that Augustine overlooked the idea of progress. A modern poet of

impious repute who, in all probability, has never read
Augustine, faithfully epitomizes the spirit of his
work, however, when he says that civilization *est dans
la diminution des traces du péché originel*. True progress, regarded from the only point of view that is of
consequence, which is the spiritual, lies in the growth
of the celestial city to the detriment of the terrestrial.

Augustine, moreover, was the originator of the
conception of *humanity* as a society composed of the
dead rather than of the living, which comprises the
future as well as the past, and is held together not
by material but by spiritual bonds.   This conception,
adopted and amplified by Comte, was destined to become, thanks to the blindness of positivism, an im-
manent and terrestrial divinity who would usurp the
place of the transcendental one; but Comte, conscious
of his obligation to Augustine, reserved a place in
his *Bibliothèque positive* for the *City of God*.

Many surprises await him who has the patience
(quickly becoming the delight) to read Augustine's
two-and-twenty books.   Many ideas which ignorant
moderns believe to be quite new are to be met
with on the pages penned by this African prelate.
Eucken writes: " On certain points Augustine, with
his powerful and deep subjectivity, is nearer to us
than Hegel and Schopenhauer."

You may have read in the *Soirées de Saint-Péters-
bourg* by De Maistre that disease does not derive from

natural causes, as is generally held, but is a consequence of sin. Perhaps this thought gave you fresh grounds for admiring the originality of the great Savoyard apologist, and we find it again, whether borrowed or reinvented I know not, in the best-known work of one of the most famous of modern English writers, in *Erewhon* by Samuel Butler, who uses it in an exaggerated form, for satirical purposes of his own. But if you open the *City of God* you will find it stated in Book XXII that, besides the many other ills that beset mankind, disease also is one of the forms of punishment we have earned by our sins.

The matter can be carried further still. Look, for example, at chapter xxvi of the eleventh book, and you will find the following: " We are, we know that we are, and we love both our being and our knowing. In these three things . . . no aspect that is false disturbs us, for they are not as things that exist outside ourselves, that we touch with some bodily sense . . . but are free from all fallacious phantasms or images of fancy; I possess the absolute certainty that I am, that I know my being and love it. In possession of these truths I do not fear the arguments of Academicians who say: ' What if thou dost deceive thyself? ' If I deceive myself then I *am*. For he who is not cannot be deceived, and therefore if I am deceived, I am. Then, if it be I who do deceive myself, how can I deceive myself? "

Who can fail to recognize in this passage, written more than twelve centuries earlier, the famous *cogito ergo sum* of Descartes? The starting-point of that pretentious modern philosophy which, little by little, has merged being in thought and God in man, is but a theft from Augustine's work, and, like all ill-gotten gain, has injured both the thieves and the receivers. Augustine himself was an idealist, but his is not the idealism that developed with Descartes and Kant, that deifies man, and reduces the universe to an act of human thought. For him also to know and to be are indeed one and the same thing, not in man, however, but in God. " *Et nulla natura est, nisi quia nosti eam.*" No thing is, save in so far as it is known to Thee, O God!

From every point of view Augustine's thought is theocentric. The history of mankind, which had previously been regarded as the result of chance, of climate, of human passions and necessities, was shown by Augustine to depend upon the acceptance or non-acceptance of God; and human vicissitudes, which seem to us the most important things in the universe, and of which we are foolishly proud, are really, as Augustine has demonstrated, but brief and bloody episodes occurring between the creation of light at the beginning of time and the creation of the new Heaven of the resurrected.

CHAPTER XXIX

THE LAST PHASE

IN 426, as soon as the heavy task of writing the *City of God* was completed, Augustine entrusted the material and external duties of the bishopric to his friend Heraclius, whom he persuaded the other bishops and the people to accept as his coadjutor and successor. At the same time he again addressed a request to the Christians of Hippo which he had already proffered some years before—that they would grant him at least five free days every week in order that he might have leisure to attend to the many appeals that reached him from all sides. A year of recapitulation followed during which he had time to get his breath and begin writing a new book he had long had in mind, which was to be a sort of critical review of all he had accomplished in the course of forty years. From 386 until 426 he may be said to have done little else but write, and now that the chief monument was completed he felt the need of again going over the road he had travelled, of examining even those insignificant huts he had constructed with hands that were still unskilled while in the Brianza region. In such a mass of writings— Augustine counted them and found their number to be two hundred and thirty-two, several unfinished and others missing—he might well discover some wherein he had fallen into error, had used unsuitable language, or even contradicted himself. In the two volumes of the *Retractationes* he revised ninety-three works in the order of their writing, twenty-six composed before he was made bishop and seventy-seven afterwards. A third volume should have followed, but he was not granted time to finish it.

We must not conclude, however, that it was because he was weary and wished to lay down his pen that he chose a helper and begged to be allowed some leisure. Such was not the case, for in the four years of life that remained to him he continued as heretofore filling tablets and covering sheets of parchment with his writings. He was a saint indeed, but the demon that possesses the writer he never succeeded in casting out! It is true that, unlike ourselves, his motives in composing and publishing were not those of greed or the desire for fame; he wrote from an apostolic necessity, in compliance with the requests of others and as an act of charity. For many years now he had been a pillar of fire in the Church, a pillar upon which Catholics looked with a happy sense of security and strength, and which filled heretics with dread not only in Africa but throughout the Christian world. He was a tongue and a pen in the service of God, and speak and write he must to the very end. Some saints help mankind by their secret prayers, others through suffering cheerfully endured,

18

and others again by the performance of the most
repugnant acts of mercy; upon Augustine the gift of
language had been bestowed, and by his word he
served millions.

He was now seventy-two, but his eyesight was excellent, his pulse steady, his mind clear, and his great
heart ever overflowing with love, and so, year after
year, new works were sent forth from his cell at
Hippo.   In 427 the *Speculum de Scriptura,* a learned
syllogism of Bible texts, appeared, to be followed in
428 by the *De Hæresibus* dedicated to Quodvultdeus,
a history and criticism this of all known heresies down
to the Pelagian, and by the *Tractatus adversus Judæos.*
In that same year, 428, there came to Hippo with
the Gothic militia an Arian bishop, Maximinius by
name, whom Augustine's coadjutor, Heraclius, chal-
lenged to a disputation.   But the aged bishop himself
was obliged to enter the arena, first, however, having
exacted a promise from Maximinius that he would
either await a rejoinder or acknowledge himself in
error.   But the Arian did not keep his word.   For
one whole day he harangued and then left for Carthage without waiting for Augustine's reply.

Augustine composed two short works on the subject of this episode, entitled respectively *Collatio
cum Maximinio* and *Contra Maximinium.*   But he
was not done with polemics.   The Semi-Pelagians of
Gaul continued in rebellion against the Augustinian

doctrines of predestination and grace, which seemed
to them too harsh and inhuman, and in the course of
the years 428 and 429 Augustine wrote his *De Prædestinatione Sanctorum* and *De Dono Perseverantiæ*,
both addressed to Prosper of Aquitania and Hilarius.
Moreover, that champion of Pelagianism Julian of
Eclanum would not leave him alone.   Augustine had
already confuted his arguments in 421, in his *Contra
Julianum*, a work in six volumes, but Julian had
replied with a violently libellous work in eight
volumes full of vituperation against the Bishop of
Hippo.   Augustine was not to be silenced, however,
and set about composing a third work against Julian,
which is known as the *Contra Julianum Opus imperfectum* because its completion was prevented by
Augustine's death, which took place while he was
engaged on the sixth volume.

But another and final storm was about to descend
upon him.   In 410 those who had fled before the
fury of Alaric's onslaught had considered Africa a
place of safe refuge from the barbarians.   In May
429, however, a horde of eight thousand Vandals and
Alani under Genseric landed in Mauretania, and after
invading and devastating that region, passed on into
Numidia.   Ever since the year 420 the Vandals had
been encamped in southern Spain, but they probably
would never have invaded Africa had they not been
summoned by one who at Carthage was actually the

representative of the imperial power—by Count Bonifacius himself.   The man, who was jealous of
Aetius, was opposed to Placidia, who was governing in
the name of her son Valentinian III.   He would not
go to Italy to justify his attitude, and, attacked by
the imperial forces, he summoned the Vandals from
Spain in his defence.   When he saw how formidable
was the ally he had brought into the country—a terrible enemy indeed rather than an ally, whose one
thought was to massacre, plunder, and burn—Bonifacius, influenced also by letters from Augustine,
made his peace with Placidia and turned his arms
against the barbarians.   But it was too late. Genseric
and his horde were already masters of the country;
only three cities still remained in the hands of the
Romans—Carthage, Cirta, and Hippo.   Bonifacius
shut himself up in Hippo and Genseric laid siege to
the town.   The siege lasted fourteen months, and
finally Hippo was destroyed by fire.   Augustine did
not witness the downfall of his city, for he had died
in the preceding year, but he lived long enough and
saw enough to cause him acute suffering until the
end of his days.

The Vandals — all either pagans or Arians —
respected nothing, not even the churches.   Rather
than a war this was but a bloody onslaught by eight
thousand wild beasts let loose.   Possidius relates that
Augustine " passed the last most embittered and sor-

rowful months of his old age seeing churches bereft of their priests and ministers, pious virgins and those who were vowed to chastity dispersed, some of these dying in torment or succumbing beneath cruel blows; others he saw losing the life of the soul, the body's purity, even their faith itself, and ending as the slaves of merciless masters. Hymns and the divine songs of praise to God were no longer heard in the churches; in many places sacred edifices were consumed by fire, the solemn sacrifices to God were forbidden and banished from their altars; the sacraments were no longer invoked or were invoked in vain, for the ministers were all dispersed. Forests, rock-fastnesses, and caves no longer afforded safe refuge, and some who resorted to them were captured and slain, while many others perished from hunger." Further and still more awful details may be found in the sermon *De Tempore Barbarico,* by the deacon Quodvultdeus, who later became Bishop of Carthage.

Many bishops had sought refuge in Hippo, and wept and prayed with Augustine, who must certainly have meditated upon the strange destiny which had thrown him among heretics in his youth, had kept him combating heretics for forty years, and now obliged him to look for defence to the soldiers of Bonifacius, nearly all of whom were heretics, here in this Hippo of his which was surrounded by the heretics of Genseric himself. Probably never since

the days of his trial at Milan had he suffered as in
those months.

One day, when he and his companions were seated
at meat, he suddenly exclaimed: " Listen and hear
what I ask of God in these unhappy times; either that
He deign to deliver this city from its enemies or, if
that may not be, that He give us strength to bear the
weight of His will, or at least that He remove me
from this world and take me to Himself." It would
appear that the Lord heard his prayer, for a few days
later he sickened of a fever and never again rose from
his bed.

Augustine was seventy-six years of age, and it was
a miracle that he had lived so long. He had never
enjoyed perfect health, but had been delicate from his
childhood. He had his first severe illness almost in
infancy, when he was in danger of death. He often
spoke of a *pressus stomachi* or *dolor pectoris* which,
judging by symptoms he mentions, we may conclude
was due to asthma. Hardly had he reached Rome
when he fell a victim to malaria; at Milan in 386 he
again had trouble with his chest, and his asthma was
aggravated by an attack of bronchitis which tortured
him during his holiday at Cassiciacum and gave him
an honest excuse for relinquishing his professorship.
He was very unwell during his entire holiday in the
Brianza country; he could speak neither aloud nor
at any length, and to reprimand Licentius or Tri-

getius was an undertaking which exhausted him. Even to write for any length of time wearied him, and he feared indeed that his life was threatened.

In the early days of his conventual life at Tagaste he wrote to a friend that his delicate health was a great hindrance to him, and at a later date he wrote to another friend that he could not walk, sit, nor stand, so great was the pain caused by hæmorrhoids, that scourge of those who lead a sedentary life. Years afterwards, in the course of a sermon he told his listeners that he was indeed already old in years, but that ill-health had long since aged him prematurely. Yet this sufferer from asthma, bronchitis, and malaria survived for more than three-quarters of a century, working assiduously and sparing himself never. Holiness and the pursuit of literature prolong life; the two extremes may be observed in Anthony the Hermit who lived for more than a century, and in Fontenelle—like Augustine delicately constituted but in all else his opposite—who lived to be a hundred.

Augustine did not fear death, yet even when he desired it he did not seek it. Like all who have really achieved much he felt he had not accomplished enough, that he had still to finish work begun. His answer to Julian was unfinished, the greatest mystical commentary on the Old and New Testaments was incomplete, in part indeed was as yet only roughly planned; the Arians were still to be converted, and a

thousand other projects were to be carried out which
sleepless hours brought back to his ever-active mind.
Therefore, when a certain man came to his bedside and
begged for his blessing on a sick relative, that he
might be restored to health, Augustine's answer was:
" My son, did I possess such power I would begin by
healing myself." But the sick man insisted, saying
that he had been told in a vision to go to the bishop,
who would place his hands on his head and cause him
to be healed. To satisfy him Augustine laid his
feverish hand upon the young man's head, praying to
God the while, and the dying saint's prayer was
answered.

Eleven days before his death, conscious that the
fever was increasing in violence, Augustine gave
orders that no one should enter his room save his
physician and those who brought him his food. On
the threshold of that perfect bliss which had been
the supreme desire of his whole life, he wished to be
alone with his God and to spend the time in prayer.
When the doctors forbade him to weary himself with
reading he caused several of the penitential psalms to
be copied out in large letters on broad sheets of parchment and hung opposite his bed that his eyes might
always rest upon them; and as he meditated upon
these verses his tears flowed freely.

And so one evening, while the bishops and some
friends were praying beside the narrow bed on which

he lay, his heart ceased its beating and his great soul, freed from the worn-out machine of bones and flesh, soared upwards at last to revel in that Divine Contemplation to which he had aspired for more than forty years.

This day of this third birth was the 28th August of the year 430.

While his brethren were chanting the psalms in the chamber of death the drunken Vandals beneath the walls of Hippo were howling like wild beasts, in their impatience to put the city to sack.

" He had made no will," Possidius tells us, " for this poor man of God had nothing to leave." A treasure of immense value he did leave indeed, but one which thieves cannot steal nor Vandals destroy.

CHAPTER XXX

THE GREATNESS OF AUGUSTINE

SAINT AUGUSTINE is one of those for whom death does not exist.

I do not mean this with regard to himself and the truer second life, but with regard to ourselves and to this life wherein for a time we dwell as guests. I mean that he is ever present and living here below as if he had never died, so that, after studying him for a time, we receive the impression of having known him and conversed with him, of having been his friend. His bones are divided among many places both in Europe and Africa, but his spirit enjoys the double privilege of dwelling in Heaven in the light of God's countenance and of remaining upon earth to shed light on us—a warm light, a fiery light, for the secret of his survival is love. All celebrities survive in the memory of their works, but this is usually a national memory and not one of affection; they are present in statues, in books, and in our brains, but they are far from our hearts.

Augustine's, on the contrary, is an actual, intimate, almost tangible presence, and our admiration for him is steeped in affection. Augustine, to use a homely phrase, " steals affection," *ruba il bene*. Should we meet him to-morrow face to face, we feel that after saluting his episcopal ring, we should wish to kiss his cheek as if he were a friend come back or a father risen from the dead.   I, at least, feel thus towards him.   I admire him with all the strength of my intellect, with the Church I venerate him as a saint, but more than this I love him with all the devotion of which my heart is capable.

This is why he is one of the very few who have never left us, who live on, one might say, beside us. The reasons for this twofold immortality are not difficult to understand.   He is indeed blessèd, because he is the guest of God, basks in His presence, and shares in the supernatural; but there is in him also the man, the man complete, a man like one of us, whom at times we see transfigured and resplendent in the celestial city, but in whom also we never fail to find the brother who has known miseries like ours, who has wept as children weep, who fell in love like any other adolescent, who knew friendship as we did in our youth, who was proud as we are proud, who sank deep in the pit of which the mire still defiles us, and who still shows us the way of escape and stretches out to us his firm, warm hand.

There are saints who in the beginning were almost criminals, and others whose childlike innocence was never impaired.   The majority of men, however, have not sunk to actual criminality, but, on the other hand, have allowed their early purity to be defiled. Augustine is like ourselves.   Before achieving sanctity he belonged to the majority. His sins were those common to the greater number—love of woman, of gain, and of fame. From these sins he freed himself, but only after a hard struggle, and it is the fact of this struggle that shows us how strongly rooted was his humanity, and that brings him still nearer to us. For we ourselves—those of us at least who do not live like certain insects that revel in filth—are creatures fighting to rid our spirits of the scabs left by original sin, and to reach the heights to which Augustine attained. He succeeded where we as yet have failed, but to know that in the beginning he so closely resembled us inspires the hope that we may also resemble him in his victory, and this consoling thought increases our affection for him. We find, furthermore, that some residuum of the old man remained with him always, or at least for a long time after his conversion, and this discovery, which does not prejudice the completeness of his sanctity, makes us love him all the more devotedly because, after scaling the heights, there still remains with him some remnant of that wherewith he was clothed in the low country. Thus do we see him still as our brother who has not lost all the resemblance he bore to us, and who, while exhorting us to strive upwards, encourages the hope that to reach him is not impossible.

He heartens us by showing us that conversion is not deprivation but sublimation. We do not destroy the tree to plant another (which in the case of the soul would be an impossible undertaking), but we prune it, clean it, and engraft it, that it may grow taller and yield finer fruit. Augustine's sensuality was sublimated into the yearning for spiritual bliss; his desire for happiness into quiet repose in Divine Wisdom; his passionate attachment to individuals into loving charity for all; his pride into the ambition to recreate in himself the lost image of God and to be united to Him, to become an atom of His glory. What he accomplished by distilling from the poison of evil the healing draught of goodness why should not we also be able to accomplish?

To compare ourselves to Augustine is certainly presumptuous, but to endeavour to imitate him is a duty. If in some ways he is our brother, in many others he towers above us, not only because of his saintliness, but because of his immense genius. Joseph of Copertino and Benedict Labre are examples to prove that sanctity may be co-existent with ignorance, even with a certain want of intelligence. In the eyes of God genius and knowledge are by no means demerits, but alone they are insufficient. When, however, we find a saint who, besides all the virtues of sanctity, is yet a man complete and possessed of boundless wisdom and unlimited genius, we cannot refrain—we men of the pen at least—from offering him, together with our affection, our very hearty admiration.

Most men are but mutilated beings, only parts of men; " mere sketches " Emerson has called them; and Kierkegaard (for once strangely optimistic) adds that it takes two of them to make one. Ibsen goes farther still, saying: " I see only paunches, heads, and hands, but no longer any man on earth." Let us question another deserter concerning the integrity of the ideal. " *L'homme parfait,*" Renan writes, " *serait celui qui serait à la fois poète, philosophe, savant, homme vertueux, et cela non par intervalles et à des moments distincts (il ne le serait alors que médiocrement) mais par une intime compénétration à tous les moments de sa vie . . . chez qui, en un mot, tous les éléments de l'humanité se réuniraient, comme dans l'humanité elle-même.*" Such a complete, perfect, and rare man was Augustine, and he was something more besides, for to all the highest attributes of humanity he added the supernatural seal of sanctity. We extol the many-sided men of the Renaissance and marvel at Leonardo, who was a scientist and a painter, an engineer and a poet, an architect and a sculptor. Indeed, we may well admire him, yet among his attributes metaphysical contemplation, moral perfection, the mystical sense, and the heroic exemplification of life are lacking.

In Augustine nothing is lacking; he is all things. He is the whole man, the universal man, the man without a gap. Besides being a man he is a superman,

not in Nietzsche's sense, but in that of St. Gregory
the Great; one of those men *quia qui divini sapiunt
videlicet suprahomines sunt*, supermen in so much as
they are acquainted with things divine. And this
not because Augustine is a poet, orator, psychologist,
philosopher, theologian, and mystic, but because he
unites in himself, in harmony of synthesis, all those
contrasting elements which in most men cause crises,
error, and conflict, and in him, on the contrary, bring
forth a higher truth.

He is first a sinner and then a saint; first a professor, then a pastor; but afterwards at the same time
he is a cenobite and an executive (in his capacity as
bishop), a poet and a rationalist, a dialectician and
a romantic, a traditionalist and a revolutionary, an
eloquent rhetorician, and a popular orator. At times
he seems to us a Socrates, intent upon dividing and
subdividing the several meanings of words; at times
he seems a Pindar who, amidst impassioned digressions,
sings of the victories of the inner paradise. Sometimes he inveighs against riches and property as if
he were an anarchist, only presently to admonish
Christians to respect all Governments, even the most
evil. He seeks inner enlightenment through the
soul's impulse towards God, but lays such stress upon
the power and need of the Church that he arrives at
the point of declaring that he believes in the Gospels
because the Church commands him to do so, and not

in the Church because the Gospels bear witness to her. He is a pessimist who sees humanity as a *massa damnationis* or *massa perditionis,* yet he is so thoroughly optimistic withal that he preaches happiness to the very end as the true object of man, and declares it to be obtainable, inasmuch as he identifies bliss with God. He stresses the necessity for reason in order to achieve comprehension of the dogmas of the faith, but at the same time he recognizes that faith alone can help us to comprehend. " *Intellige, ut credas, verbum meum; crede ut intelligas, verbum Dei.*" The author of the *Liber de sancta Virginitate,* who was ever the champion of chastity, is the same who recognized the necessity for prostitution: " *Aufer meretrices de rebus humanis, turbaveris omnia libidinibus.*" The same author who so subtly sets forth the free will of man proceeds to scandalize most people by his theories of predestination and grace. At times he argues and disputes like any lawyer, and again, becoming the mystic, he soars to the heights of ecstasy. He intercedes for his enemies and seeks the condemnation of heretics. In him abstractions and lyricism, logic and charity, dominate in turn, one completing the other without producing inner conflict.

Alone perhaps even among Catholics he achieved in himself that fusion of the elements which, although seemingly antagonistic, are nevertheless necessary in order to attain to perfect adequacy of experience for the world, of thought for the universe, of the individual for humanity, of man (in so far as this is vouchsafed to him) for God. Unilateral minds are subject to error and sterility. He who is all intellect and pure logic is the prisoner of formulæ, of syllogisms, of abstract terminologies, and has no hold on reality, which in its entirety is irreducible to concepts. Intelligence when it exists alone is not even capable of understanding. He who is all heart loses himself in diffusive outpourings; he who is merely intuitive and impulsive may have moments of wonderful insight, but he will always end in uncertainty or be led into heresy by self-esteem. He who considers only externals and forms, discipline and the letter of the law, runs the risk of becoming either a Pharisee or a bigot. He who trusts only in himself and in his personal experience ends as a Lutheran; he who gives himself up exclusively to mechanical forms of devotion ends as a Tibetan monk. Extremes are always dangerous when the spirit is dominated by one alone; when they work together they become fruitful.

This miraculous collaboration existed in Augustine. In him opposites, even the most pronounced extremes, were not destroyed and did not destroy, but they generated and built up. A tree cannot live without its bark, but were it all bark it would die. Bare and twisted roots hidden in the earth are in appearance the opposite of fine leafy branches and of flowers that

19

bask in the air and sunshine; but were it not for the
roots the leaves would not unfold, and the roots by
themselves would remain barren sticks.

It is the same with the Church; without the living
flame of love and revelation the grand cathedral
wherein we shelter would never have been built. Had
the cathedral never been built, that fire, exposed to
all the winds that blow, might have been extinguished.
But if we consider only the innumerable architraves,
pilasters, and buttresses of the edifice, and allow that
original flame to expire, the Church becomes merely
a pile of lifeless masonry. He who sees one side, and
that side only, is in error; he who respects that dualism
which is indispensable attains to truth. Half solu-
tions are mediocre, but if they contain the extremes,
and all of the extremes, a synthesis is reached which
is not compromise but transcendence. And it is
thanks precisely to this rich complexity of his spirit,
wherein the most diverse tendencies were united, that
Augustine was able to become the most Catholic, that
is to say the most universal, of the Doctors of the
Church.

In his mind opposites did not give rise to sterile
self-conflict, nor did they rest inert in outward con-
ciliation and juxtaposition, but out of their positive
coexistence and their convergence towards a fruitful
conjunction truth arose. One of the secrets of Augustinian genius lies in the fact that his nature harboured

all extremes without allowing itself to be dominated by one alone, and forced them to co-operate towards a discovery by which they were transcended.

Augustine was opposed to every unilateral excess. Against Origen, who held that all men would be saved, he maintained the doctrine of predestination for a few of the elect; against Pelagius, who relied almost entirely on the power of man's will, he preached the mystery of Grace; against Jovinian, who, eleven centuries before Luther, believed in faith without works, he declared the necessity for active charity; against the Manichæans, who regarded evil as invincible, he maintained that the world was good when it left the Creator's hands; against the Donatists, who boasted that they alone possessed sanctity, he preached that humanity is divided between two cities which contain both the righteous and sinners, and that they shall dwell together until the last day. He was always for integral truth, never for exaggeration, and still less for compromise.

At times his thoughts may appear paradoxical and even hazardous and his style too full of those antitheses which seem to verge on the absurd. All those who have dealt with matters of profound thought have exposed themselves to this criticism. He who seeks to express the inexpressible falls into apparent *agudezas*, and he who would think what is unthinkable, skirts paradox. Just as the sublime is but a step

removed from the ridiculous, so high metaphysics
are but a step removed from the absurd, and lofty
mysticism is but a step removed from heresy. Whoever goes to the depths of a question and announces
something new is constrained to make use of expressions that may seem mere quibbles or paradoxical con-
tortions. Before condemning such expressions in
Augustine it should be remembered that we find
similar phrases in the Gospels themselves, as when
Jesus says that he who would save his life must lose
it, but that he who shall have lost it shall save it; that
He is come into the world that the blind may see
and those who see become blind; that to those who
have shall be given and from those who have little, that
little shall be taken away; that he who is raised up
shall be cast down and he who is cast down be raised
up. Here we are confronted with expressions divinely
exact and of profound significance, but with all the
appearance of paradox.

Thus the doctrine of predestination, which of all
Augustine's theories was the one most severely condemned and which appears to place Grace and Free
Will in positions of irresolvable opposition, is set forth
at times in language which seems to do violence to
ordinary logic by the performance of dialectical
feats of equilibrium which are disconcerting. But
it must be remembered that he is dealing with mysteries, and with unfathomable mysteries. To assume

that all men shall receive effectual Grace, that is to say salvation, is to limit the omnipotence of God; to deny the possibility that all may render themselves deserving of recompense is to limit man's freedom, which is God-given. Augustine, seeking to reach if not the explanation at least the comprehension of such deep mysteries, was forced to resort to formulæ which at times offend our common sense and, what is worse, lend themselves to the corroboration of error. But if we keep in mind his entire system of thought without taking from it or exaggerating any one element as certain heretics have done, we shall see that the whole links up harmoniously, and that the strangeness of his expressions cloaks thought that is subtle indeed but at the same time lucid and precise.

With regard to predestination, for example, it must be remembered that Augustine realized most keenly the vast distance that separates man from God. God created man and man may become reunited to God, but only after such reunion will he be able to understand Him fully and to plumb the depths of the impenetrable. For the present, in spite of all heretical boastings, we continue to maintain that man is not God and is incapable of understanding God. What to man with his limitations appears injustice may be a higher justice in the eyes of God; man's pride is offset by the example of unequalled humility which the Almighty gave in the person of Christ. Thus

the doctrine of predestination, in which many see an
offence against God's loving-kindness, may be but a
further proof of His mercy. According to Augustine man is most free when he chooses what is good
and strives towards it. True liberty, he holds, does
not consist in being able to do either good or evil,
but in freedom to choose the good and forsake the
evil. " When is free will freer than when it cannot
serve sin? " he asks. Now God desires for all men
what is good, and in their striving towards what is
good He helps them by the gift of His Grace, and
thus furthers human liberty in the sense described
above, as charity, the love of perfection, and the
hatred of evil grow ever greater. The more
He influences man by directing him towards
righteousness the greater does He render man's true
liberty.

All that can be urged against Augustine therefore
is but the outcome of his profound thought, of his
greatness itself. If some, isolating a single principle
without regard to the rest, and forcing it to the point
of absurdity, have fallen into heresy, the fault is not
Augustine's. Everything that is sublime is dangerous.
" That which cannot be abused is of little value in
use," was said by an Englishman, if I mistake not.
Rabelais took the Augustinian formula " *dilige et
quod vis fac* " and made it the motto of his Abbey
of Thélème: " *Fais ce que voudras*," thus making

Augustine appear the father of Epicureanism or even of anarchy. But one sees at a glance that the curate of Meudon has decapitated the phrase, has deprived it of the word of greatest importance—*dilige*—love. Augustine meant that when a man deeply loves his fellow-men he may do as he likes, because he possesses supreme truth and blessèd charity and cannot err, but he had no intention of justifying the materialism of Panurge and his companions.

Luther, for example, took Augustine's ideas concerning the power of faith and the merits of Christ and overlooked all his exhortations on the subject of works of charity and of our duty to strive for salvation; by mutilating Augustine, Luther made him, with St. Paul, responsible for his own errors. Calvin and Jansen separated Augustine's reflections on predestination from their context, neglecting his remarks on free will, and pretended to establish the heresies that bear their names on the authority of the orthodox doctor. Augustine does indeed teach that we must give ourselves up to the love of God, but in the sense of being disposed to receive His mercies, not in that of inaction and passivity, and he teaches that prayer must alternate with good works. Can he then be justly accused of being the father of quietism?

Heresies also are necessary, as St. Paul said, and if certain heresies made use of Augustine, of one who fought against heretics for forty consecutive years, we must see in this abuse a fresh proof of his inestimable greatness.

The same answer may serve for those who inveigh against certain peculiarities of his style which they regard as rhetorical vices or as coarseness. In the first place ordinary people, who are generally cold by nature, fail to understand, even when they are intelligent, the fervour of an ardent soul, and mistake for mere rhetoric what is but the natural form of thoughts which translate the richness of the heart by the richness of eloquence. Despite the fact that he is a professor and a German as well, Adolf Harnack has reached a fuller understanding of this matter than have all the throng of the coldly fastidious. "There exists a prejudice against rhetoric," he says, "and wherever it appears people feel bound to cry out against it, declaring it to be but a mask for insincerity. But like poetry rhetoric is an art. I will go even further and say that it is itself a form of poetry, and in ancient days true sentiment was free to use it as an instrument without fear of encountering disapproval." Augustine was a very great writer, at times even a poet, and in him not all that appears to be emphasis or affectation is attributable to his habit of rhetoric. Such expressions as "*copiosæ inopiæ et ignominiosæ gloriæ*" or "*pudet non esse impudentem*" or "*vitam mortalem an mortalem vitalem*" or "*loquaces nuti*" or "*inimica amicitia*" and the like

impress us as cunningly contrived antithesis, but
when they are restored to their context it generally
becomes apparent that they were needed to give per-
ceptible force to the thought.   And those bold images
that cause sterile pedants—whose opinions are really
of no account—to twist their foolish faces, such as
" *memoria quasi venter est animi,*" " *abigo ea manu
cordis a facie recordationis mea,*" " *ore cogitationis,*"
" *aure cordis,*" and many more, may be found in language equally bold in the Bible, in Homer, in Shake-
speare, and in all great writers who create without
regard for restrictions set up by manuals and by
common sense.

Those who know Augustine only through even the
best of translations can form no adequate conception
of his literary genius.   His style is not always uni-
form: now it is pathetic and soulful like romantic
prose; now flowing in solemn periods, sonorous and
incisive, like Cicero at his best; now calm, simple,
and definite, like a Platonic dialogue; now like Tertullian drastic and impetuous.   Not only was he the
greatest theologian and philosopher of his time but
also the greatest writer.   Although he is infinitely
better in the *carmen solutum* than in the *carmen
vinctum* he is also a poet, and at times a very success-
ful poet.   Compare him with the most famous Latin
writers of his day, with the learned Macrobius, with
that composer of resounding mosaics, Claudianus, and

you will find that at the close of the fourth century and the beginning of the fifth, this African was the sole representative of the great art of Latin prose, and endowed its ancient majesty with a deeper meaning and a cadence that is entirely modern.

Certainly not all of his works are of equal value. They contain, following closely one upon another, polished, brilliant pages mighty in their power and loftiness, and pages that convey the impression of muffled rumblings in a head working like a volcano that is not extinct but only in a phase of inactivity— that seethes indeed, but does not overflow its crater.

But when the moment of eruption comes what light it brings! St. Paul advanced by means of a succession of disconnected explosions; Augustine's ideas burst forth all together, and he did his best to put as many of them as possible into sonorous words and language that not infrequently suffered violence at his hands. But words are what they are—finite like every material thing, whereas thought possesses the infinitude of things spiritual. At times therefore Augustine grew tired of writing, indeed almost despaired, because he was never satisfied with his work. Among other forms of tragedy he experienced that which the true artist knows, the tragedy of the eternal Pygmalion surrendering before the unconquerable inflexibility of matter.

The secret of his greatness both as a writer and as

a thinker is that he lived what he thought and felt deeply what he said.   To him God was not a conception to be acknowledged, but a living reality to be enjoyed; truth was not merely a thing to be learned, but a treasure of which he burned to possess himself, a part of his daily sustenance; Christianity was not a mere collection of doctrines, but a life that must be lived to the full.   He referred the most transcendent problems to his own ego, made theology a part of his being, melted pure thought in the furnace of his heart, soared freely in the realms of ideology but always with wings of flame.   Beneath his serene universality there lurked ever a trace of personal controversy, a shadow of autobiography.   In describing the union of the human and divine in Christ he used as a parallel the union of the body and soul in man; to illustrate the Trinity he cited that inner trinity of the human soul: *esse, nosse, velle.*   And for this appeal of his to the inner experience of the individual as well as for his feverish unrest, he may well be termed, albeit with all due reservations, the first Romantic of the West, the first modern man. Petrarch, whom many regard as deserving this definition, was but a disciple and follower of Augustine.

Moderns, however, do not resemble him in what is essential in him—his mysticism. Augustine is not only a learned exegete, philosopher, and theologian, but also, and first, a mystic. The ecstasy of Ostia

was not the only one he experienced. Many years
later he confided to God: " At times Thou dost bring
me to a state of strange and sweet plenitude of I
know not what delight, which, should it attain its
highest point, would become something no longer of
this life."   No one since St. Paul has defined the
mystical Christ as clearly as Augustine. His spirit,
avid of happiness, could find satisfaction only in God,
that is, in the fullness of eternal bliss of which he had
tasted some infinitesimal part here below in his communion with the ever-living Christ.   And so strong
was his consciousness of our brotherhood with the
Crucified Lord that only to bear this life of ours,
to " carry our own mortality," seemed to him, as he
expressed it in a sublime figure, to be bearing the
cross like Him who conquered death: " *Tollit quo-
dammodo crucem suam qui regit mortalitatem
suam.*"

The great thinker and the great theologian were
strong in him, but what was to him of supreme importance was to love God and cause Him to be loved.
In the midst of the most thorny and intricate of controversial encounters, if the thought of God entered
his heart, his hand would tremble and his whole being
quiver with an almost intolerable sense of tenderness
and longing. With minutest care and at all times
he manifested his devotion to the Almighty, whom
he could not clothe in garments created by his fancy

as do the simple, but Who to him was ever shrouded in mystery because his powerful intellect had enabled him to glimpse God's illimitable infinitude. Others must have images, specifications, machines. It was not so with him. He never sank into the void of abstractions, never gasped in the rarified atmosphere of the mere collector of concepts.

He did not form his thoughts into a fixed and special system—that trap set for the indolent and the simple—nor his mind into a schematic and official model. He never proclaimed as Christian doctrine what he knew to be Augustinian and all his own, and he always said what is essential in life and what is divine in Christianity—little enough, it would seem, but that little infinite and alone worthy of being considered, loved, and lived.

We see him from a distance, hallowed by the centuries, through canonization, through his disciples and a throng of commentators, and he impresses us as the intellectual sovereign of his age, the fire upon the heights, the Father of the Church, standing enveloped in his episcopal robes. But if we draw near to him and read between the lines of his sermons and epistles, we discover beside his greatness, which looms ever greater, his spiritual solitude and also his sadness.

We must not allow ourselves to be misled by the number of persons who either wrote or appealed to him. In reality he was never anything but the bishop of a minor city of Africa, a gladiator in a provincial amphitheatre. This being, who to us seems the most brightly shining light of Christianity in the fifth century, spent five-and-thirty years in a fourth-rate diocese struggling with an ignorant, troublesome, and vulgar flock, who may have loved him but were incapable of understanding him. Carthage appreciated him, and at several crises sought the support of his genius, but no one of his admirers thought of rescuing him from what was little better than exile at Hippo. He had but slight intercourse with Rome. St. Jerome tried to ignore him; the theologians of Gaul rose against him; Julian of Eclanum delighted in dissecting his work with subtle and malicious irony. We are forced to acknowledge that, in his own day, he was less highly esteemed than might have been expected, and still less was he the recipient of honours and praise such as were bestowed on many less worthy than he. Here again was a case where the eagle was sacrificed to the fowls and kept in a cage for the benefit of the peacocks.

It is impossible that one so restless should never have longed to escape from the small town where the will of the people held him prisoner. We feel also that they relegated him, perhaps all unintentionally, to comparative isolation. By birth he did not belong to the professional class of presbyters and monks. In the eyes of the clergy two circumstances of his past, connected with Manichæism and literature, still told against him. It was as if a poet who was also a freemason should suddenly become converted and succeed in entering the priesthood. The Church would take him to her heart with rejoicing and on occasion make good use of his genius and erudition, but he would ever remain an object of suspicion to sheep grown old in the fold, as one from whom a fresh surprise might be expected, and he would be watched as a falcon is watched in the midst of a flight of ducks, or the daring hero in all well-ordered societies. At bottom he remained ever, if not precisely an irregular soldier, at least one who often fought alone, with his own weapons and regardless of ancient rules, and although he always respected the supreme commander who resides at Rome and was prompt to obey him in all things, yet he was never entered on the lists for promotion. Thus and at even greater cost must superiority be purchased.

All things worked together to deepen his sadness. Surrounded not by people capable of understanding the strong and eternal leaven of his thought, but by beings who preyed upon him day by day, case by case, exacting from him information, help, sermons, defence, he was deprived of the *otium* which, in a measure, might have soothed his spirit, might perhaps have cheered it by making possible the composition of some speculative synthesis or work of art; but instead he was distracted and wearied by discord in the African Church and by the daily cares in connection with his small but troublesome flock. The finest minds of the day would gladly have held converse with him, but they for the most part resided beyond the seas, and for more than forty years Augustine never once set sail from Africa. Who then was there to comfort him but God? Who could understand and commiserate the perpetual restlessness of his spirit if not He Who had created it as it was, that it might bear witness to the Creator's power? It is because of all these circumstances that the form of his art which was most natural to him was the soliloquy. What are the *Confessions* indeed but an impassioned soliloquy in the presence of God?

The centuries alone have crowned Augustine with the love he deserved; and not until after his death was his greatness recognized, comprehended, and made clear, and it has grown steadily brighter down to our own day. His second life in the souls of Christians and in the Church is not yet ended, nor will it ever end.

The genius of Augustine works that miracle in us which was the dream of the poet Francis Thompson:

" O world invisible, we view thee,
O world intangible, we touch thee,
O world unknowable, we know thee,
Inapprehensible, we clutch thee! "

At once an eagle and a diver, he lifts us up among the constellations and guides us in the immensities of abysmal space. By his intellect we are led up to loopholes which afford glimpses of the most impenetrable mysteries, and his loving and fiery heart still, after so many centuries, finds the way to the heart of man and causes it to beat in unison with his own. For a moment we forget the Doctor of Grace and see him only as the Doctor of Charity. We recognize in him not only the architect of theology and the giant of philosophy, but also the brother who, like ourselves, has suffered and sinned, the saint who has scaled the walls of the city of eternal joy, and seated himself at the feet of the God to Whom he is reunited for all eternity.

331.   Birth of Monica, mother of Augustine.

354 (13th November).   Birth of Augustine at Tagaste in Numidia. Son of Patricius and Monica.

361.   Begins his studies under a *litterator* of Tagaste.

367.   Is sent to Madaura to begin the study of grammar.

370.   Owing to lack of means Augustine is obliged to spend a year in idleness with his parents in Tagaste.

371.   His father dies. With the help of his relative and friend Romanianus he goes to Carthage to pursue his studies.
Falls in love, and makes the woman his mistress.

372.   Birth of his son Adeodatus.

373.   Cicero's *Hortensius* is a revelation of wisdom and philosophy, but presently he becomes an " auditor " among the Manichæans.

374.   He returns to Tagaste to teach grammar.
Alypius is one of his first pupils.
His mother, finding he has become a Manichæan, will not have him in her house, and for a time Augustine is the guest of Romanianus.

375.   The death of a dearly loved friend makes him wish to leave Tagaste. Aided by Romanianus

he removes to Carthage, where he opens a
school of rhetoric.

380.   Writes his first book: *De Pulchro et Apto*
(lost).

383.   His intercourse with the Manichæan bishop
Faustus of Mileve and his disappointment.

He deceives his mother up to the last moment,
and sets sail for Rome in search of fortune.

At Rome he is the guest of a Manichæan and
is taken ill (malaria?).

He opens a school, but the pupils cheat him.

384.   Recommended by the Manichæans to Aurelius
Symmachus, prefect of the city, who sends
him to Milan as professor of rhetoric. As soon
as he arrives he visits St. Ambrose, Bishop of
Milan.

385.   His mother joins him in Milan with her other
son (Navigius).

The Panegyric of Emperor Valentinian II and
of Bautus (lost).

Monica persuades Augustine to become engaged and to repudiate his concubine.

He becomes engaged, but nevertheless takes
another mistress.

Attends Ambrose's sermons and becomes ever
more detached from the Manichæans.

386.   Studies the Neo-Platonists and discovers the
greatness of St. Paul.

Confesses to the priest Simplicianus, who tells
him of the conversion of the rhetorician,
Marius Victorinus.

386 (July). Pontitianus acquaints him with the
life of Anthony the Hermit.
The crisis of grief in the garden (*Tolle, lege*).
He renounces the second concubine, his affianced bride, and the school, that he may devote his life to God.

386 (end of August). Withdraws to the villa of
Verecondus at Cassiciacum in Brianza, with
his mother, his son Adeodatus, his brother Navigius, his cousins Lastidianus and Rusticus and
his disciples, Alypius, Licentius, and Trigetius.

386 (November). At Cassiciacum he writes his
first philosophical dialogues:
Contra Academicos.
De Vita beata (13-15th Nov.).
De Ordine.

387 (beginning of year). Begins the *Soliloquies*.

387 (early in March). Returns to Milan to prepare
for baptism. Writes the *De Immortalitate
Animæ* and begins the *De Musica*.

387 (24th–25th April). Is baptized by St. Ambrose
with his son Adeodatus and Alypius.

387 (May). Leaves for Ostia with his mother, Adeodatus, and his friends Alypius and Evodius.

387 (June?). While they are waiting for a ship at

Ostia Monica is taken ill and dies a few days later. Augustine, instead of proceeding to Carthage, stops in Rome. In the course of this year he writes:

De Quantitate Animæ.

De Moribus Ecclesiæ Catholicæ et de Moribus Manichæorum.

De Genesi contra Manichæos.

De libero Arbitrio (only the first book).

388 (August). Leaves Rome.

388. Remains for a time in Carthage in the house of the Christian Innocentius, then goes to Tagaste, where he liquidates his father's small estate, gives the money to the poor and, with a few friends, founds the first Augustinian convent.

389. Writes the *De Magistro*. Death of his son Adeodatus and of his friend Nebridius.

388–90. Writes the *De vera Religione* and begins the *De diversis Quæstionibus*.

391. *De Utilitate Credendi ad Honoratum.*

Going to Hippo Regius to convert a rich man who hesitates, by the will of the people he is ordained a priest by Bishop Valerius.

At Hippo he founds the second monastery, which will be entered by Alypius, Evodius, Severus, Profuturus, Possidius, Fortunatus, and others.

391. Writes *De duabus Animabus contra Mani-chæos.*

392 (28th–29th August). Disputation with the Manichæan Fortunatus, who disappears from Hippo. (Chronicled in *Contra Fortunatum Disputatio.*)

393 (October). Synod at Hippo, where Augustine speaks on faith and on the creed. (*De Fide et Symbolo.*)

393. *De Genesi ad Litteram* (*liber imperfectus*).
Psalmus abecedarius contra Partem Donati.
Epistola XXVIII ad Hieronymum.
De Sermone Domini in Monte.

394. His friend Alypius is made Bishop of Tagaste.

394–5. *Expositio quarundam Propositionum ex Epistola ad Romanos.*
Epistolæ ad Galatas Expositio.
Epistolæ ad Romanos Expositio inchoata.
Contra Adimantum.
De Mendacio.
De Continentia.

396. Valerius, Bishop of Hippo, appoints Augustine to share his bishopric. He is consecrated by Melagius, Primate of Numidia.
De Agone Christiano.
Contra Epistolam quam vocant Fundamenti (of Mani).

Death of Valerius. Augustine succeeds him as Bishop of Hippo.

397. *De diversis Quæstionibus ad Simplicianum.*
Begins the *De Doctrina Christiana.* Goes to the Council of Carthage.

397–8. Writes the *Confessions.*

398. Controversy with Fortunius, Donatist Bishop of Tubersicum.
Controversy with the Manichæan Felix, who is converted to Catholicism. (See *De Actis cum Felice Manichæo.*)
Begins the *Contra Faustum Manichærum.*

399. Invites Crispinus, Donatist Bishop of Calama, to a disputation.

400. *De Cathechizandis Rudibus.*
Contra Faustum Manichæum.
De Consensu Evangelistarum.
Ad Inquisitiones Januari.
De Fide Rerum quæ non Videntur.
Contra Epistulam Parmeniani.
De Trinitate.
De Baptismo contra Donatistas.

401. Council of Carthage.
De bono Coniugali.
De sancta Virginitate.
Contra Litteras Petiliani.
De Unitate Ecclesiæ (*ad catholicos epistula de secta Donatistarum*).

De Benesi ad Litteram (finished about the year 415).

404. Council at Carthage.

405. *De Natura Boni.*

405–6. *Contra Secundinum Manichæum.*

406. *De Divinatione Dæmonium.*

406–7. *Contra Cresconium Grammaticum Partis Donati.*

408. *Epistola* (XCIII) *ad Vincentium* (*de hæreticis vi coercendis*).

408–9. *Epistola* (CII) *ad Deogratias* (*Sex Quæstiones contra Paganos*).

409. *Epistola* (CVIII) *ad Macrobium* (*de non iterando baptismo*).

410. *Epistola* (CXVIII) *ad Dioscorum* (*de philosophæ erroribus*).
Epistola (CXX) *ad Consentinum* (*de Trinitate*).
The Goths under Alaric sack Rome.

411 (1st, 3rd, 8th June). Conference at Carthage between Catholics and Donatists presided over by the tribune Marcellinus, in which Augustine took a leading part. Condemnation of the Donatists.
Breviculus Conlationis cum Donatistis.
De unico Baptismo contra Petilianum.

412. *Contra Partem Donati post Gesta.*
Epistola (CXXXVII) *ad Volusianum* (*de Incarnatione*).

Epistola (CXXXVIII) *ad Marcellinum.*

Epistola (CXL) *ad Honoratum (de Gratia).*

De Peccatorum Meritis et Remissione et de Baptismo Parvulorum.

413.   *De Fide et Operibus.*

De Spiritu et Littera ad Marcellinum.

Epistola (CXLVII) *ad Paulinam (de videndo Deo).*

He begins the *De Civitate Dei.*

414.   *Epistola* (CLVII) *ad Hilarium siculum (de Pelagianismo).*

Epistola ad Julianam (de bono viduitatis).

Paulus Orosius, " presbyter hispanus," arrives at Hippo to consult Augustine.

415.   *De Natura et Gratia.*

Ad Orosium Presbyterum contra Priscillianistas et Origenistas.

Epistola (CLXVI) *ad Hieronymum (de origine animæ).*

Epistola (CLXVII) *ad Hieronymum (de sententia Jacobi).*

Ad Episcopos Eutropium et Paulum de Perfectione Justitiæ Hominis.

Enarrationes in Psalmos.

416.   Augustine goes to the council at Mileve, against the Pelagians.

In Joannis Evangelium.

In Epistolam Joannis ad Parthos.

417.   *De Gestis Pelagii ad Aurelium Episcopum.*

      Epistola (CLXXXV) *ad Bonifacium (de correctione Donatistarum).*

      Epistola (CLXXXVI) *ad Paulinum No. 1 (de Pelagianismo).*

      Epistola (CLXXXVII) *ad Dardanum (de Pelagianismo).*

      De Patientia (?).

418.   Goes to the Council at Carthage.

      De Gratia Christi et de Peccato originali.

418 (September). *Sermo ad Cæsariensis Ecclesiæ Plebem.*

418 (20th September). *Gesta cum emerito Cæsariensi Donatistarum Episcopo.*

      Contra Sermones Arianorum.

419.   Council of Carthage.

      De Coniugiis adulterinis.

      Locutionum in Heptateuchum.

      Quæstiones in Heptateuchum.

      Epistola (CXCIX) *ad Hesychium (de fine sæculi).*

      De Anima et ejus Origine.

419–20. *De Nuptiis et Concupiscentia.*

420.   Converts the heretic Leporius, a monk from Gaul.

      Contra duas Epistulas Pelagian. ad Bonifacium.

      Contra Mendacium (liber ad Consentium).

Contra Adversarium Legis et Prophetarum.

421. *Contra Julianum Hæresis Pelagianæ Defensorem.*

Enchiridion ad Laurentium.

De Cura pro Mortuis gerenda.

422. *De octo Dulcitii Quæstionibus.*

425 (?). He is at Uzali, the guest of Evodius, and preaches to the people.

426. Finishes the *De Civitate Dei.*

(26 Sept.) Gives over the care of the bishopric to his coadjutor Heraclius.

426–7. *De Gratia et libero Arbitrio.*

De Correptione et Gratia.

Retractationum.

427. *Speculum de Scriptura.*

428. *Collatio cum Maximino Arianorum Episcopo.*

Contra Maximinum.

Tractatus adversus Judæos.

428–9. *De Prædestinatione sanctorum* (*liber ad Prosperum et Hilarium*).

De Dono Perseverantiæ.

De Hæresibus ad Quodvultdeus.

429. The Vandals invade Numidia.

429–30. *Opus imperfectum contra Julianum.*

430 (June). Genseric with his Vandals and Alani lays siege to Hippo.

430 (28th August). Death of Augustine.

BIBLIOGRAPHY

The Augustinian bibliography is immense. I shall not do more than give an idea of it here.

Abundant bibliographical material may be found in:

Potthast: *Bibliotheca historica Medii Ævi.* Berlin, 1896, second edition, vol. ii, 1186–88.

U. Chevalier: *Répertoire des sources historiques du Moyen Âge.* Bio-bibliographie. Paris, Picard, 1905, i, 371–81.

E. Portalié in *Dictionnaire de théologie catholique.* Paris, Letouzey, 1909, i, 2284 and following.

Ueberweg: *Grundriss der Geschichte der Philosophie.* III. *Die Patristische und Scholastische Philosophie.* Second edition (hrsgg. v. B. Geyer), Berlin, Mittler, 1928, p. 96; pp. 663–7.

A. Casamassa in *Enciclopedia italiana.* Milan, 1928, i, 913, and following.

The most accessible edition of the works is that of Migne, *Patriologia Latina,* vols. xxxii–xlvii. The works of Augustine are in course of reprinting in the *Corpus Scriptorum ecclesiasticorum Latinorum,* Vienna (Holder). Twenty-two volumes have already appeared.

They are cited under the abbreviation CSEL. For the reader's convenience I give a list of the volumes that have already been published in this important collection.

XII. *Liber qui appellatur Speculum et Liber de divinis Scripturis.* F. Weihrich (1887).

XXV, p. 1. *De Utilitate Credendi; De duabus Animabus; contra Fortunatum, contra Adimantum; Contra Epistulam Fundamenti; Contra Faustum.* I. Zycha (1891).

XXV, p. 2. *Contra Felicem; De Natura Boni; Epistula Secundini; Contra Secundinum. Acc. Evodii de Fide contro Manicheos et Commonitorium Augustini.* I. Zycha (1892).

XXVIII, p. 1. *De Genesi, ad Litteram libri XII; eiusdem libri capitula; de Genesi ad Litteram imperfectus liber; Locutionum in Heptateuchum libri VIII.* I. Zycha (1894).

XXVIII, p. 2. *Quæstionum in Heptateuchum libri VII; Adnotationum in Job liber unus.* I. Zycha (1895).

XXXIII. *Confessionum libri XIII.* P. Knöll (1896).

XXXIV, p. 1. *Epistulæ I–XXX.* A. Goldbacher (1895).

XXXIV, p. 2. *Epistulæ XXXI–CXXIII.* A. Goldbacher (1898).

XXXVI. *Retractationum Libri II.* P. Knöll (1902).

XL, p. 1.   *De Civitate Dei libri I–XIII.*   E. Hoffmann (1899).

XL, p. 2.   *De Civitate Dei libri XIV–XXII.*   E.
Hoffmann (1900).

XLI.   *De Fide et Symbolo; De Fide et Operibus; De
Agone Christiano; De Continentia; De bono
Coniugali; De sancta Virginitate; De bono
Viduitatis; De adulterinis Coniugiis libri II; De
Mendacis; Contra Mendacium; De Opere Mona-
chorum; De Divinatione Dæmonum; De Cura
pro Mortuis gerenda; De Patientia.*   I. Zycha
(1900).

XLII.   *De Perfectione Iustitiæ Hominis; De Gestis
Pelagii; De Gratia Christi et De Peccato origin-
alis libri II; De Nuptiis et Concupiscentia ad
Valerium Comitem.*   C. F. Urba et I. Zycha
(1902).

XLIII.   *De Consensu Evangelistarum libri IV.*   F.
Weihrich (1904).

XLIV.   *Epistulæ CXXIV–CLXXXIV.*   A. Goldbacher (1904).

LI.   *Scripta contra Donatistas. Psalmus contra
Partem Donati; Contra Epistulam Parmeniani
libri III; De Baptismo libri VII.*   M. Petschenig
(1908).

LII.   *Contra Litteras Petiliani libri III; Epistula ad
Catholicos; De Secta Donatistarum; Contra
Cresconium libri IV.*   M. Petschenig (1909).

LIII. *Liber de unico Baptismo; Breviculus Colla-
tionis cum Donatistis; Contra Partem Donati
post Gesta; Sermo ad Cæsariensis Ecclesiæ
Plebem; Gesta cum Emerito; Contra Gauden-
tium libri II.* M. Petschenig (1910).

LVII. *Epistulæ CLXXXV–CCLXX.* A. Goldbacher (1911).

LVIII. *Epistulæ: præfatio editoris et indices.* A.
Goldbacher (1923).

LX. *De Peccatorum Meritis et Remissione et de Bap-
tismo Parvulorum ad Marcellinum libri III; De
Spiritu et Littera; De Natura et Gratia; De
Natura et Origine Animæ libri IV; Contra duas
Epistulas Pelagianorum libri IV.* C. F. Urba et
I. Zycha (1913).

LXIII. *Contra Academicos libri III; De beata Vita;
De Ordine libri II.* P. Knöll (1922).

Father Germano Morin, in forty years of patient
research, has discovered fifty-one new sermons by
Augustine. Some of these are contained in a volume
he has published: S. *Aureli Augustini Tractatus sive
Sermones inediti.* Campoduni (Kempten), Kosel,
1917.

My quotations from the *Confessions* are taken from
the De Labriolle edition (Paris, Belles Lettres, 1925–6,
2 volumes).

The only ancient biography of Augustine is that

of Possidius, *Vita Augustini* (in Minge, *P. L.*, xxxii, 33–66), which has been frequently reprinted. The most modern edition is the following:

Weiskotten, H. T., ed. *Sancti Augustini Vita scripta a Possidio Episcopo*. Edited and revised text. Princeton University Press, 1919 (with notes and an English translation).

An excellent guide in the study of Augustinian thought is the volume by E. Gilson, *Introduction à l'étude de Saint-Augustin*. Paris, G. Vrin, 1929. (At the end a good bibliography, not complete but orderly.)

M. Grabmann, *Die Grundgedanken der hl. Augustinus über Seele und Gott*. Kole, 1916 (second edition, 1929), is a valuable but brief essay.

I am most heartily grateful to Father Antonio Casamassa, O.S.A.—one of the most profound students of St. Augustine of our times—and to Don Giuseppe de Luca, who helped me with information and advice.

Under the auspices of Father A. Casamassa there will be published in Rome, on the occasion of the fifteenth centenary of the death of the saint, a *Miscellanea Agostiniana*, which will contain essays by students from every country.

INDEX

Abelard, 240

Academicians. *See* Plato and Platonism

Adeodatus, 46, 107, 117, 121, 123, 125, 167, 190, 197, 209, 216–17

Adimantus or Addas, 234

Aetius, 276

Africa, Roman, 14

Africans, sensuality of, 17

Alani invade Africa, 275–7

Alaric, 258–60, 261, 262

Alexander the Great, 120

Alypius, 64, 67, 86, 107, 118–21, 145, 146, 150, 153, 154, 156, 157, 163, 167, 169, 171, 173, 175, 183, 190, 191, 209, 212, 224, 228, 234

Ambrose, 90, 91, 109, 110, 129, 138, 149, 191; influences Augustine, 16, 46, 92, 93–106, 108, 114, 137, 159, 170, 175, 181, 187–9, 206, 240, 247; hymns of, 177, 184, 185, 198, 219

Anthony the Hermit, 121, 221, 279; influences Augustine, 19, 145–50, 152, 156, 211

Antidicomarianites, 231

Antigonus, bishop, 65–6

Apuleius, 15; influences Augustine, 19, 35–9, 131; quoted, 39

Arcesilaus, 86, 132

Arians, 103, 109, 110, 137, 142, 148, 184, 274, 276, 279

Aristotle, 37, 120, 248; *Categories* of, 77–8, 140; influences Augustine, 77–8

Astrology influences Augustine, 38, 69–70, 78, 130–1

Athanasius, 20, 100, 146, 148

Attalus, Priscus, 259

Augustine, appearance of, 48; pictures of, 10

Augustine, character of, 11, 160–1; charity, 214, 285; dual nature, 27–8, 41–2, 63, 143–4, 161–2, 265–6; greatness of, 282–305; pride, 61; sadness, 303–4; sensuality, 18, 23, 27, 40–6, 119, 143–4, 152, 161–2, 254–6, 285; vanity, 45

Augustine, family of: sister, 117, 192, 211, 212; mistress, 45, 46, 107, 117, 121–6; second mistress, 125. *See also* Adeodatus (son); Monica (mother); Navigius (brother); Patricius (father)

Augustine, influences on. *See* Ambrose; Anthony the Hermit; Apuleius; Aristotle; Astrology; Bible; Cicero; Manichæism; Neo-Platonism; Paul, St.; Plato and Platonism; Plotinus; Pontitianus; Porphyry; Simplicianus; Symmachus; *Tolle et lege*; Victorinus

Augustine, life of: chronology, 306–15; birth, 20; childhood, 20–33; baptism delayed, 21, 33–4; early education, 31–2; adolescence (education interrupted), 40–6; young manhood, 47, 83; later education, 48–54; the *Eversores*, 48–9; desire for marriage, 43–5, 114–26, 136–7; "first conversion," 47–54; professor of rhetoric, 67–165; death of friend, 71–2; ill-health, 84–5, 162–3, 278–9; meets drunken beggar, 107–13; betrothal, 114–26; "second conversion," 127–34; complete conversion, 151–61; baptism and confirmation, 187–9; made priest, 222–4; made